Book of
Anna

Book of *Anna*

Stella Kuzyk Noble

XULON PRESS

Xulon Press
2301 Lucien Way #415
Maitland, FL 32751
407.339.4217
www.xulonpress.com

Printed in the United States of America.

Paperback ISBN-13: 978-1-6322-1517-8
Hardcover ISBN-13: 978-1-6322-1518-5
eBook ISBN-13: 978-1-6322-1519-2

Table of Contents

Dedication

I dedicate this book to Pauline Kuzyk Sartorio, my 102 year old sister and second mother to the Manitoba Kuzyk family clan. She is my mother's second oldest girl and Anna relied on her and referred to her as her "little mother".

Author, Stella Kuzyk Noble

Preface

I wrote this book as a eulogy to the person that I have always loved and admired the most, my mother Anna Zabiaka Kuzyk. I did not want her life and memory to be lost like so many others due to the passage of time. The book acknowledges the sacrifices and hardships she endured while raising and providing for her 16 children beginning over 100 years ago. I wish to thank my sister Pauline for her contribution by providing details and incidents of the earlier years described in this book. I wish to thank my son Gary as well for helping with the research and for his work creating and maintaining the Kuzyk and Zabiaka family tree, tracing the family lines back over 250 years.

Book Summary

The Book of Anna chronicles the life of Anna Zabiaka Kuzyk. It shares her struggles, her joys and her heartbreaks during the 101 years of her life from her early years in the Ukraine, raising her family in Manitoba and her final days in Hamilton Ontario. She first met her future husband, Metro Kuzyk, in the village of Volkivtsi, County Borschiv, Galacia, under Austrian rule at that time, where they were both born and raised. When she traveled to Canada with her father, brothers and sister, she met up with Metro again and married him. They had 12 of their children reach adulthood, all being born in Manitoba, all with families and all successful in their own right.

This book explains the difficulties that pioneer immigrants faced, blazing trails, clearing ground, scratching out a living and trying to survive in the difficult climate and conditions of rural Manitoba 100 years ago. Through prayer, determination, hard work, sacrifice, generosity and love, not only for their family but neighbours as well they not only survived, but were successful in providing better lives for their children and their children's children.

Many of us would not be here today if it weren't for women like Anna. She had the heart of a lion and the ferocity of a lioness protecting her brood. She gave birth to 16 children. When Anna passed away at the age of 101 in 1990 she left 10 children, 31 grandchildren, 45 great grandchildren and 3 great great grandchildren.

CHAPTER 1

Oh Canada!

Anna was born of Ukrainian parents, Gregory (Harry) and Anna Zabiaka in the small village of Volkivtsi, County Borshchiv in the region of Galicia in the Ukraine, at that time under Austrian rule, on May 25, 1888. It was a beautiful area near the Carpathian Mountains. She was one of five children living, as her mother had several miscarriages. She was named Anna after her mother.

Anna's mother had passed away when Anna was only 11. This left her with many responsibilities. As she grew older her interests were quite obvious. She was an actress and she sang and acted in all the plays at the local theatre. She was blonde and strikingly beautiful. Anna's sister Dora also sang and performed in plays, but the boys were crazy about Anna.

Her father was a wealthy man. He was a bee keeper and owned an orchard. He was considered to be a man of means in his village. He was also a drinking man and enjoyed going to the pubs on the week-ends to meet with his cronies and discuss politics.

Anna's brother Fred met a young widow and they fell in love. They were soon married and had four children, Sophie, Nat, Nick and Lena. One day his wife received a letter from her previous in-laws in Canada. They would pay for Fred and his wife to come to Canada with their four children. When Anna heard about this, she became very excited and asked her brother to take her along too. She promised that she would work hard in Canada to repay him for her fare. She decided to talk it over with her father.

Anna discussed the situation with her father. He decided that since her mother had died at such an early age, there was nothing left for him or his family to keep them in the old country. Her father decided to sell the orchard and embark on a journey to Canada. He had heard so much about Canada from friends and relatives who had immigrated prior to his plans of moving, that he decided it would be nice if his family joined them as well.

Anna was about to turn 24 when the family travelled by train to Hamburg Germany in early May, 1912 to board the S.S. Campanello for their trip to Halifax, Nova Scotia, Canada. It must have been somewhat frightening because only two weeks earlier, the Titanic had sunk in these same waters. Many experts agree that the Campanello was the famous "mystery ship" that was seen by the Titanic but they unfortunately were unable to make contact with it. The Campanello, later renamed Flavia, would be sunk as well by a German torpedo only six years later.

It was a glorious time for all of them and the excitement was mounting everywhere. Her father was nowhere to be found however, as they waited to board the ship. Anna's sister Dora was becoming tearful and even brothers Fred and young Philip were getting anxious. Father had their boarding passes and the time to board was fast approaching. Meanwhile their father had boarded and was happily chatting with some of the local folk who were also going to Canada. He was oblivious to everything else. Anna, who spoke a little German, managed to make herself understood by one of the stewards who had her father paged and he finally appeared with their boarding passes. So they set sail to a new country and a new beginning.

SS Campanello

Chapter 2

Wedding Bells

They arrived in Halifax on May 13, 1912 and then travelled by train on to Winnipeg Manitoba. Subsequently they decided to settle on a homestead near Fork River. Fred and his wife moved in with her previous in-laws, the Solomon's. They eventually obtained a homestead of their own. Some months later, Anna's father thought that Anna, going on 25 years old, was well past her prime for marriage.

He knew of a handsome young bachelor who was homesteading on a farm just across the road from his son's place. The bachelor was from the same village. He approached the young man to marry Anna. The young man's name was Metro Kuzyk. He was very handsome with red hair, freckles and dark brown eyes. Back in the old country he had always had feelings for Anna and so it was arranged that they be married as soon as possible. Anna did not object. They were married by Reverend Kinish in St. Josaphat's Church in Sifton Manitoba on Feb. 2, 1913.

For her wedding, Anna wore her hair short and curled. It was parted on the right side. As it was a cold wintry day and Anna wore her usual kerchief over her head for the picture taking outside. Her face was oval, with high cheek bones and she had a very distinctive pug nose below her green eyes. She wore a long ankle length brown skirt and a white shirt embroidered with red and black cross stitching. She also had on a pure white, full length half apron over her skirt. This was the traditional garb worn by the Ukrainian girls on their wedding day. Her feet were trim in a brand new pair of high button shoes.

Metro was handsome in his black suit and tie, red wavy hair, straight nose with brown eyes and a clean shaven face. Later, they had a photograph taken of the entire wedding party. They also had a photograph taken of the bride and groom. They made a handsome couple.

Anna's father, Gregory Zabiaka, who went by Harry, decided to move in with his son Fred and his wife on the homestead one farm over from Metro's and Anna's place. He also helped Anna and Metro by setting them up with a team of horses as their wedding present. Harry would live there until his death at the age of 87 in 1932.

Fork River was approximately three miles from Metro and Anna's place. It was about twenty miles from the nearest larger town of Dauphin, Manitoba.

Anna's sister Dora married a young man who worked on the railway and she moved with him to Swift Current, Saskatchewan. Anna's brother Philip married Nellie Chornoboy and they decided to move to the United States.

Anna was a very passionate and religious person. She dreaded thunderstorms. Whenever an electrical storm struck she would get out her rosary, kneel down and pray reverently.

Anna was also a very self-assured and confident woman. She was also a proud, strong willed individual, to the point of being dominant. She may have been just under five feet tall but when she became angry, she was like a fireball. Later, when she was upset with Metro, she would not hesitate to pick up a broom or anything else that was handy and threaten him with it menacingly just to make her point. Metro, on the other hand, although he was about six foot tall, was quiet and passive. He was warm and when he smiled, a dimple would appear in his left cheek. He was six months older than Anna. He was born on October 31, 1887. He seldom argued with Anna and for the most part, he let her have her way.

Anna and Metro Kuzyk Wedding Feb. 2, 1913

Chapter 3

First of the Brood

The house was relatively new. A big two storey place, constructed out of logs. The sleeping quarters were upstairs. A large cooking wood stove was in one corner of the downstairs. A pine dining room table was situated by the window in the southern part of the house with two long benches on either side of the table. There was a root cellar with a trap door at the eastern portion of the house. In the centre of the downstairs area, there was a huge buck stove, longer in length than height, which was used specifically for heating the house.

The winter was cold with temperatures falling well below zero degrees Fahrenheit. Metro would hitch up the horses to the sleigh and go into the bush to chop wood for heating the house. Anna spent most of the balance of the winter months working on her cross stitching and feeding the chickens and pigs.

Anna was with child and her activities were limited but this did not prevent her from doing her part in helping Metro. Although she was petite, she was strong and healthy and when it came to working outside, she could do the work of any man.

The barn was in the back of the house. The chicken coop was much closer and a large granary, also constructed out of logs, was in the front of the house. At the present time it was empty but Anna knew come spring she would be busy filling it up for the following winter.

Anna was already saving all the feathers from the chickens in preparation for the pillows and feather tick she was working on. She would spend hours stemming the feathers and saving them for her tick. On

Sunday afternoons, she would position herself beside the stove and work on the stemming of the feathers while Metro read her a love story about the old country from the weekly Ukrainian newspaper he received. This was her favourite time of the week.

Sadly, Metro was not always at home during the winter months. On occasion, he would hop the freight cars and go into Dauphin to do odd jobs and chop wood for the locals to make extra money. This would leave Anna at home by herself to tend to the chores. Metro always made sure she had plenty of chopped wood for the winter. He learned to speak English very quickly while Anna did not have the same opportunity to learn to speak the English language. Anna could neither read nor write in any language.

There were some nights when Anna felt extremely lonely. She would sit by the stove while stemming her feathers by the light of the coal oil lamp, and listen to the timber wolves howling outside. When she would get up to throw some wood into the fire, she would follow her shadow and this gave her a very uneasy feeling. Sometimes it seemed as though the wolves were just below the window or at the door. She would prop a chair up against the door to give her that extra security. In the mornings she would do a head count of the chickens to make sure they were still all there. She worried that the wolves or fox would get them during the night.

On one of Metro's trips home, he and Anna's brother Fred shot a deer out of season and hung it in the closet above the stairs for a week. Later they shared the deer meat and Anna's father told the story about the small doe he had shot in the old country. How he was warned that the gendarmes were coming to investigate the shooting. He hid the small doe in the cradle and sat down and slowly began to rock it. When the gendarmes arrived and checked the place out, they found nothing and never thought to look in the cradle. Everyone laughed half-heartedly, as they had heard this story many times before.

Spring came early and Anna was excited. They had made plans for the spring seeding. There was wheat to be planted and the garden as well had to be ploughed and seeded. The neighbours would help each other out, including Anna's brother Fred. Anna especially looked forward to the garden. She loved to get her hands into the soil and work with it. She felt closer to God at this time of the year.

She spent a great deal of time clearing the field of the stones. The piles of stone seemed endless. Some of the rocks were quite large, but this did not deter her even though she was expecting. She would wear a large linen apron and carry the smaller rocks in it to the clearing.

She started to build her pyatz. It was an outdoor oven. She would gather horse manure along the road. She needed this as the horse manure acted as an adhesive to the mixture. She would place the manure in a sack and bring it home to combine it with clay and water, adding straw as needed and work it with her bare feet in a wooden box until the desired consistency. The floor of the pyatz she laid with brick. Metro went into the woods and cut down some small birch saplings. These were very pliable and Anna placed them eight inches apart in an arched position the full length of the pyatz. Some chicken wire was then placed on the outer and inner part of the oven ready for the clay. She would then apply the clay to the wire frame of the oven. It was arched, about twelve feet long and four feet wide with an open grate beneath it for the firewood which would heat the oven. The opening was closed up with a steel door propped up against the oven itself. Metro made the hoe-like instrument which Anna would use to pull the loaves of bread from the back of the oven to the front. In the old country, they also used the pyatz for sleeping in. Sometimes on a cold night, the oven would be ideal, because the fire would still be smouldering and would keep the individual warm during the night.

It was getting near her time and there appeared to be an urgency in everything Anna did. She seldom walked, but instead almost ran. She hurried with the garden and dug up the potatoes, carrots, beets and cabbage. Metro unloaded the vegetables into the root cellar. It was a good harvest and Anna felt almost driven to get all the vegetables into the house.

She also had the granary stocked. The cucumbers had been picked and were sitting in a wooden barrel covered in brine. Her sauerkraut was also in a crock covered with a clean cloth. Metro loved his sauerkraut, especially in the perogies.

It happened during harvest time. Anna began to have severe labour pains towards the end of September. Metro dropped everything, hitched up the wagon and took off for the midwife. Anna did not want him to go. She did not feel she wanted to be alone at this time. She also knew Metro was very reluctant to be the only one present at her side when the baby came. So he left and she waited for them to return.

Metro became a father on the 18th day of September 1913. It was a boy and they named him Michael. Anna attempted to breast feed the baby, but her milk was not sufficient for the child. They needed a cow and, fortunately, with the money from the harvested wheat, they managed to buy a cow. However, they would have to suffer many hardships during the coming winter months.

Anna's Pyatz

Chapter 4

Teacher's Pet

Anna gave birth to her second son the following September 15, 1914. They christened him Andrew. He was born just twelve months after Michael. Anna had her hands full. Once again, it was harvest time and she was needed by Metro to assist him, but he knew this would not be possible. The midwife had been there to help Anna with the birth. The boy was healthy and Anna thanked God.

Metro and Anna went into Dauphin and registered the birth of Andrew and of their first son Michael. Later this would create a big problem because it was on record that Michael and Andrew were born the same year, one month apart and were, therefore, twins. Actually, this all came out when Michael applied for his old age security and received a year's retroactive pension when it was proven that he was born on September 18, 1913.

While in Dauphin, Anna and Metro received their Naturalization papers. It had been two and one half years since Anna arrived in Canada and now she had two sons and she had become a Canadian citizen.

Anna's father would come by to visit with them and he would tell Metro to keep his wife in check by giving her a good beating once in a while. Anna thought back to the old country and her own mother. The physical abuse that was inflicted upon her mother by her father every time he came home from the pub in a drunken stupor. Anna would nurse her mother back to health. She was not disrespectful to her father when he spoke of beatings, but she quietly resented him for it.

The roadway through the yard was used by all of the locals as well as by many other folk to get to Fork River. It was a convenient short cut. It was about a mile through the property before one entered the dense bush. This property was government owned. The bush was used for firewood by most of the farmers in the area. There was a half a mile of this bush through which ran a pathway established by use of wagons and horses. Then one had to go for another half mile on a dirt road, which when it rained, became a muddy and rutted lane way. The main highway consisted of a gravel roadway into the town of Fork River.

One day Anna was doing some chores and happened to be in their front yard when a young woman came by in a fancy horse and buggy. She seemed to be a very nice lady as she chatted with Anna, who invited her inside and they had a good visit. She told Anna she was a school teacher. The young woman could see the lean and meagre furnishings in the house. When she spotted the infant she made a big fuss over Andrew and picked him up. She fell in love with him immediately. Anna was extremely proud.

Anna was pregnant again and she told the teacher so. Not being able to have any children of her own the teacher asked Anna if she would consider selling the baby Andrew to her. She offered Anna four hundred dollars for him. She pointed out to Anna that she already had Michael and was expecting another child, she would hardly even miss Andrew. Four hundred dollars was a great deal of money to Anna. The money would probably set her and Metro up for a long time. Anna did not know how serious the woman was but she was adamant. Anna became very possessive and refused to have anything to do with the sale of the little baby boy. She quickly retrieved the child from the school teacher's arms and held him close to her bosom.

Eleven months after the birth of Andrew, on August 26, 1915, Anna gave birth to a little girl. They baptized her Mary. The infant was very sickly and Anna was quite worried about her new daughter.

Metro built a cradle that hung from the ceiling over the bed so that Anna could just reach out at night and rock the cradle if the baby cried.

One day when Andrew was about a year old, Michael and he were playing together in the house. Anna left the infant Mary in the cradle and went to the barn to do her chores. She knew she would not be long and was not concerned. When she returned to the house she found Andrew crying and screaming. The child had puckered up his lips and was blowing in an out rapidly between screams of pain. Anna quickly asked Michael what happened. She found that Andrew had been thirsty. He had asked Michael for a cup of water. Michael had managed to open the can of kerosene, poured the kerosene into a cup and had given it to Andrew to drink. Andrew was screeching by this time and Anna was at a loss as to what to do. She ran across the road to her brother's farm and found her father at home. She explained quickly to her father what had happened. He instantly grabbed his jacket with some scotch mints in a paper bag and rushed with Anna to her place. He took the situation in and straightaway pulled out the bag of scotch mints he carried in his pocket. He gave one to Andrew to suck on. The coolness of the mint relieved the burning sensation the child was feeling and he calmed down somewhat. The baby had diarrhea for a couple of days, but nothing more serious occurred from the incident. Once again, Anna thanked God and her father for the mints.

Mary was still a sickly child. She was physically very slow. She also seemed to be favouring her legs. Anna was gravely concerned about her baby daughter. She required a great deal of care and attention. She took up a lot of Anna's time.

Anna was expecting again the following spring. She prayed often for the health of the child in her womb. On March 4, 1917 Anna gave birth to another son. Both Anna and the midwife examined the child thoroughly to ensure his health and Anna thanked God for a perfect little boy. They took the child into Fishing River and had him baptized Fred after Anna's brother.

Gregory (Harry) Zabiaka

Chapter 5

First Steps

Anna and Metro's cow was in heat so they had to contact a farmer with a bull. They finally located one about four miles away. He said he would be glad to oblige them. The fee would be a good sized pig. Anna and Metro agreed to his terms. Metro placed a rope around the cow's neck and trudged along the road to the farmer's place. Anna was anxious to start raising her own cattle. She had visions of a brighter future. Visions of grandeur. A farm with lots of cattle. Then she thought about the milking aspect of it and immediately came back to reality. There would be too much additional work involved. Metro returned from the farmer's place in the late afternoon. The deed had been accomplished and the cow was serviced.

Anna was expecting again that winter. It was a cold and blustery day in February when Anna started to get labour pains. Metro was not at home, he was out chopping wood. She was fearful that he would not get back in time to go and get the midwife. The snow was coming down heavy and Anna positioned herself beside the window and waited for Metro to arrive. It was late afternoon and she knew that it was almost time for him to come home. The sleigh appeared with Metro walking fast behind the team. Anna breathed a sigh of relief as she waited for her husband to unhitch the team and take them to the barn. There was no time for the midwife. When Metro came into the house Anna was already in bed writhing in pain. She told Metro to get the hot water which was on the stove, and told him what to do. She held on to the bed as she moaned and pushed. It was a fairly easy birth and Anna was thankful. She gave birth to her second little girl. The baby appeared to be healthy when Anna examined her. The date was February 24, 1918. It was the first time Metro assisted Anna alone in the birth of one of his children. He was in awe of the whole matter. They named the little baby Pauline and Anna was happy to have another girl. Pauline was the 5th child in five years.

Sometimes when Anna and Metro had the time they would try and get to church on Sunday. Metro would hitch up the team of horses and they would ride into Fishing River. It was a very small community with a church. There was mass said once a month and Metro and Anna would attend as often as they could. It was quite a distance to travel but closer then Fork River.

Metro was working in the field one day. It was a busy time for him. There were a lot of rocks to be cleared from the ploughed land. There were several large piles already sitting on the edge of the area he was working on. He missed Anna's help, but he knew she too was occupied with the five small children.

Anna was expecting again and her heart was heavy. She sighed as she knelt down to wash the clothes. The wooden tub was on the floor and she was kneeling beside the tub scrubbing a sheet on the washboard. The boys Michael, Andrew and Fred were outside playing. Pauline was asleep in the cradle upstairs. Anna was keeping her eye on Mary, who was thrusting herself forward around on the floor. Although Mary was three years old, she still could not walk, but merely pushed herself around on her stomach.

Anna had convinced Metro to take Mary to see an old woman who was a folk healer. The old woman poured the hot liquid wax over Mary's head into a pan of cold water. Then when the wax hardened, she would remove it from the water and read the results on the reverse side of the solidified wax. It was like reading tea leaves. The old woman advised Anna that the wax had been blessed. At the same time she poured the wax she was praying and invoking the name of Jesus. Anna and Metro had taken Mary to see the old woman three times and Anna had great faith in what they were doing. She believed in folk medicine and everything associated with it. Anna was also very superstitious.

Anna occupied herself with thoughts about Mary, as she continued to scrub the sheets. She blamed Metro partly for the sadness in her heart for the little girl on the floor. She was born just ten months after Andrew and this was far too soon. She believed Mary's condition was in some way, a punishment she had to endure.

She went to check on the boys and returned to the tub on the floor. She sighed as she got down on her knees and began to scrub the sheet again. Mary sidled up to the tub and Anna gasped and held her breath. Mary slowly lifted up one little hand and grasped the top of the tub. Then she lifted the other hand and gradually stood upright beside the tub. She was a bit unsteady on her feet and teetered. Then she started to move herself around, all the while holding on to the wooden tub for support.

Anna dropped everything. Her emotions ran high. She dashed out the door all the while screaming Metro's name over and over again, her arms flailing, as she ran for the field. Metro could hear her euphoric cries as she ran toward him. He figured something had happened. He dropped the rock he was carrying and ran towards Anna.

"Its Mary, Metro. Its Mary, she is walking," Anna screamed, gasping for breath. Together they raced back towards the house. Anna had no inkling as to what might have happened if Mary had by chance fallen into the tub of water in her absence. It was later that this notion had occurred to her, but at the time she was so overjoyed she did not give it any thought.

She believed that it was the old woman who, in God's name, was responsible for Mary starting to walk. She and Metro knelt down and thanked God. There was a great deal of joy in both their hearts. Mary was a normal child after that and learned to walk very rapidly. It was a miracle and no one could convince Anna to the contrary.

Anna went to visit the old woman a week or so later. She was so grateful to her. Anna was intrigued with the wax ritual and she also asked the old woman to teach her the art of pouring the wax and reading the reverse side of it. The old woman agreed and thought that Anna would be a good candidate to take her place when she passed on. She taught Anna everything she knew, including all the prayers said during the ritual. But she warned that anything Anna did should be done in the name of Jesus. Anna was a good student and learned well.

Winter Transportation in Mossey River

Chapter 6

Death in the Family

That winter Anna gave birth to another son. He was born on Dec. 2, 1919 and he too, like the others, was a healthy baby boy and Anna thanked God again. They called their new son Bill.

Anna got her garden in as usual the following spring. Metro got his wheat planted and they were thankful for the help they received from the good neighbours.

Michael was going on six years old. He would not be starting school until the following September. Anna relied on Michael a great deal even at such a tender age. He was her baby sitter and he did a good job.

One day Anna and Metro had to go into town and they took the infant Bill with them. She left Michael in charge and told him to look after the younger children. The boys were always into her cucumber patch. They loved to pick and eat the cucumbers. Anna made a point to tell them to stay out of it because there were snakes in the patch.

Upon their return from Fork River, to Anna's dismay, she found the cucumber patch in shambles. She was devastated. She inquired of the boys as to what had happened. Michael and Andrew told her that they got sticks and killed all the snakes in the cucumber patch. They proudly told Anna that she need not worry any more about the snakes. Anna shrugged and realized that the whole thing was rather comical. She had brought it all on herself after all. She had very few pickles that winter for the table.

During the summer months Anna would go into the bush and pick wild mushrooms. She would make mushroom soup and the children loved it. She would add fresh cream to it and the soup was rich and thick. Anna would make a big pot full and it would last for a couple of days. She knew which mushrooms were the good ones and which she should not pick.

Anna relied on Michael all the time. She could not rely on Andrew like she could on Michael whenever she had to go anywhere. It was during the hot summer that it happened. Baby Bill was six months old. He was a beautiful baby and Anna had just fed him. She handed the infant to Michael to burp while she attended to other matters. Michael was sitting in a chair. He lost his balance and dropped the baby on the floor. He fell on top of the child. Bill started to scream and cry in pain. When Anna picked the child up she knew that something was dreadfully wrong.

She kissed and hugged the baby tenderly. She told Metro that he should go see about getting the doctor to come and examine the infant. In her heart she knew that the doctor could do nothing to save the baby Bill. She would not lay the child down but walked the floor with him for two hours, whispering softly to him. She was heartbroken.

The child was quiet and limp and did not appear to have any energy left in him. He was barely breathing. Anna prepared herself for the worst. At first she refused to let go of the child. Finally she handed Bill over to Metro and decided she would prepare the baby's bottle. In that instant the child died in Metro's arms. It was too late for the doctor to do anything.

Anna retrieved the child from Metro's arms. Slowly, she began to rock back and forth and she began to wail. At the same time she cried out to God. The wailing was a haunting sound as it permeated throughout the house. It sent chills up and down the backs of the entire family. The wailing continued for about ten minutes. Gradually it subsided and Anna began to cry softly. There was an eerie silence as the children held their breath and everyone mourned Anna's great loss quietly.

Later Anna said that the baby would not die as long as he was in her arms because of her tremendous love for him. He could not die and this is what kept him alive. She guessed he died from internal injuries. They buried the infant Bill and Anna's heart was heavy with sorrow. It was nearing harvest time again and she was busy with her garden and the other children. She also prayed a great deal.

They got their harvest in that fall. Anna was occupied with all the things to do before winter set in and this somehow helped to ease her pain and sorrow for the baby boy she had lost. Her concern had to be for the living and there were five of the small children to be concerned about.

It was a strong wind blowing this winter day and Anna kept Michael home from school. A blizzard was raging. Anna was afraid to send Michael the 2 and 1/2 miles to school in the blowing storm. She went into the barn to milk the cow and left the children alone in the house. Upon her return to the house, she smelt something burning. The smoke was streaming from the oven. Upon checking the oven, she found her wedding shoes, the new pair of leather high button shoes all shrivelled up and ruined completely. The stench was overwhelming.

When she asked the boys what happened to her shoes, she found that Andrew had wanted to go outside and play in the snow. He had taken her shoes and put them on. He had gone out in the storm to play and got the shoes soaking wet. Worried as to what his mother would say if she found her shoes all wet, he decided to place them in the hot oven to get them dry and had forgotten all about them. Anna was in a dilemma. She was very upset and ready to punish Andrew. She stood there for a moment and considered the situation. They were, after all, only a pair of shoes and she could always get another pair if she wanted to. She scolded the child but did not punish him. Andrew was happy about that.

Anna was the disciplinarian in the family. Right from the start Anna made herself understood to Metro. She would discipline the children and he was not to touch any of them ever.

The following spring Anna once more got her garden in as early as possible. She was expecting in May and was rushing to get everything done before the child arrived. On May 22, 1920, Anna gave birth to another girl. They baptized her Jessie and she too was a healthy baby girl for which Anna praised God.

That summer Anna and Metro decided that they needed some pigs. They had slaughtered the old sow and needed a pig for breeding purposes. The only thing they had left to barter for the pig was the stove. They got several pigs for the stove. Anna decided that she could do her cooking outside in the big pot and did not need a stove for the summer in any event.

Anna's sister Dora came down to visit Anna and her family that summer. Because her husband worked for the railroad, she was allowed to travel free of charge on the train and would come down to visit as often as she could. When she surveyed the situation, she realized that Anna had no stove to cook on. She decided to buy her sister a stove. She was fairly well to do and could afford it so she ordered a stove from the store in Fork River and Metro and Anna went to pick it up. Anna was happy with her new stove and grateful to Dora for it. Dora also bought Anna some tin plates as everyone was eating directly from the big pot. Anna did not have any dishes to speak of in the house. With the small children, Dora decided to buy the tin plates because they could not be broken.

The following summer Dora once more came down for a visit to see Anna and her family. Once again she found Anna cooking outside on an open fire in the big pot and once again, they were eating directly out of the pot. She inquired of Anna as to what happened to the stove and the tin plates. Anna told her that the children needed milk so she had bartered the stove for a cow and a good bargain it was too. As for the plates, the boys had been playing with them and were flipping them into the air and watched them soar. They eventually lost all of the plates in the bushes. Dora gave up and shortly left for Swift Current. She decided not to invest in any stove or plates again and left Anna and her family to make do with what they had.

Anna was expecting again in the fall and the year was 1921. She gave birth to her fourth son on September 3 and they named him John. Anna was very tired and unable to help Metro with the chores. She was very appreciative that her brother Fred lived nearby and helped Metro whenever he could.

Metro, Anna Kuzyk with her Brother Fred Zabiaka

Chapter 7

Kuzyk Music

True to form the next year Anna was pregnant again. She was approximately two months on the way. It was during the winter time and she was going to the barn to milk the cow. She slipped on the ice in front of the house and fell. She immediately knew something was wrong. She managed to get up and make her way into the house. She felt it almost instantly. She was having a miscarriage. Metro happened to be at home and she thanked God for that. He prepared the hot water and looked after Anna for a couple of days until she could get back on her feet again. Later Anna said she thought it was another boy. She had some holy water in the house. She had baptized the fetus and gave it a name but she did not divulge what the name was. It was early 1922.

One day Michael was flipping through the newspaper his father had been reading. He spotted a picture of a violin in it. He became very enthused about it. For a small price, the advertisement read, one could own a violin just like it. Michael cut out the ad and approached his mother about purchasing it. Anna was not impressed at first but Michael persisted and eventually Anna gave in and had him fill out the form and mail it to the manufacturer.

A few weeks later, they were notified that the violin had arrived and was at the post office for pick up. Anna and Metro rode into Fork River to pick up the violin. When they arrived home, Anna unpacked the box and brought out the violin. It was in a very nice case and Anna examined it for flaws. Michael was at school and Anna could hardly wait to see his face when she would give the violin to him. When Michael arrived home from school, Anna proudly presented the violin to him. He was joyous. His eyes lit up like a Christmas tree and he immediately began to try and play it. Anna did not know how to play it and could not teach Michael. He would, however, listen to his mother as she hummed a tune and would attempt to play it on the violin. He became very good eventually and Anna was overjoyed with his progress. She said her son was naturally talented and bragged about his abilities to her neighbours.

Someone heard about Michael's talents. One day Anna was approached by her cousin's husband Bill Demcheson. He said he had a musical instrument for sale and asked if Anna would be interested in buying it. Anna's ears perked up as she thought about her younger son. She asked the man what kind of an instrument was it. He explained that it was called a cymbali in Ukrainian. It was a large stringed instrument which was placed on one's lap and the strings were struck with a set of wooden type pegs all over the instrument. Anna asked him to bring the cymbali down and she would look at it.

A couple of days later, Bill Demcheson brought the instrument in a large case over to Anna's place. Anna listened to the man as he played the cymbali. She immediately decided that she would have it. She recognized the instrument as being one played at her own wedding. It was large and probably too big for Andrew but he would grow with it. They agreed on a pig for the instrument and Demcheson promised to show Andrew how to play it as an added bonus. When Andrew got home from school that afternoon, he was overjoyed with the news. Anna had actually purchased an instrument for him as well. Bill explained that it was a small version of the real thing. However, it was one he had made himself and it was very old. He had made a larger one for himself and, therefore, this one was for sale. Mr. Demcheson showed Andrew how to play one easy song and Andrew caught on immediately. The rest of the children wanted to play it as well and they called the little wooden pegs piglets because the tip of the pegs resembled pig's ears.

Bill Demcheson would show up every other night and teach Andrew how to play the cymbali. Andrew was quick to learn. Anna was ecstatic. She began to spend a great deal of time with the boys, teaching them some of her old country tunes. She would hum along with them as they struggled trying to keep to the melody. It was sometimes, not very pleasant to listen to but it got better with time and they were soon playing songs of their own that they learned from school.

A year later, on October 8th, 1923, Anna gave birth to her fifth son. She wrestled with herself as to what she should name him. She was superstitious as to whether or not to name him Bill. She really liked the name. She finally decided to go against her first intuition. She would christen him Bill in any event. She was warned by the Godmother that she should not have two boys named Bill in one family. Anna did not heed her warning. She had the same Godmother and Godfather for all the children, so the Godmother knew about the death of the first Bill. They rode to Fishing River to baptize the infant where all the children were christened shortly after their birth.

Bill was a healthy bouncing baby boy and he was a beautiful child. Anna was very cautious with him at first and extremely careful leaving him alone with anyone. For a long time she watched over him like a mother hen. Eventually, she let up on her cautious ways and resumed her daily chores as usual.

Anna could not breast feed any of her children. She had attempted to breast feed but did not have sufficient milk. She envied the women who could. There was one neighbour in particular who came to visit Anna. She had a three year old boy who she was still breast feeding. The children would stand and stare in wonder watching him suckling his mother's breast. Anna was embarrassed to let her children watch but she did not say anything to the woman.

As time went by, the boys got better and better with their music. Anna was very proud that the boys were so talented and praised them constantly. She was very happy to always have music in the house. Metro was non-committal.

Anna's father would come down for a visit quite often. The boys would play him a few songs. He was very impressed and praised the boys for their efforts as well. Anna would just hum along with them and by the smile on her face, one could tell how happy she was for her sons.

The boys continued to practise on their instruments. They were getting to be very good at it. Andrew was big enough to hold the instrument entirely in his own lap while he struck the strings with his wooden pegs. Mr. Demcheson also taught Andrew how to tune the cymbali. The two boys would often play for Anna while she stemmed her feathers. She was very pleased with herself for her initiative.

One day Anna heard about a Hawaiian guitar that was for sale. Anna decided to look into the possibility of purchasing it for her children. She brought it home too and pretty soon the other children were all taking turns playing it. It had a bar across the top of the neck of the guitar. Pauline soon took to it like a fish to water and Anna was again very proud of her children.

During the winter months Anna also did a great deal of sewing. She would save her sugar and flour bags. Then she would cut an opening in the sack for the neck. Next she would cut openings for the arms. Anna would then neatly sew the hemming around the openings to give it a finished look and also to keep it from fraying. Sometimes she would add a belt to the sack and try the finished product on the girls. These were their dresses and they would have to wear them to school. They washed well, required no ironing and lasted for a long time.

Anna did not have any clothes for the younger children who did not go to school as yet. She could not afford to provide them with clothes. As a result, the younger children usually ran around naked both in the house and outside. Even during the cold winter months, they would be naked and Anna could see no harm in this. The children were used to seeing each other naked and were not curious.

One day as Anna was stemming her feathers and listening to the music, a thought occurred to her. She was making some moonshine for their own consumption. Mainly for medicinal purposes only or if company arrived. Why not make it on a larger scale and sell it to the local farmers she speculated? With this thought in mind, she immediately went to Fork River to purchase the copper piping and began to assemble a still for her moonshine.

Anna and Metro Kuzyk

Chapter 8

Blizzard of '24

That winter Anna was pregnant again. She had just finished plastering a house for one of her neighbours. Her garden had been productive and the older children helped her get the vegetables into the root cellar. The harvest had been a good one and Anna and Metro were pleased with the money they received for the wheat.

It was November and the snow had fallen early. Anna and Metro had attended at the Mowat School to hand in their secret bid on the school contract to supply wood. The other farmers were there as well. The school needed wood for the winter and the bidding on providing the school with 13 cords for the winter season had been submitted by all the farmers present at the school. Metro won the bid and the contract had been awarded to him.

Metro was out chopping the wood on a daily basis. He worked hard and long hours until darkness descended. The chores were left to Anna and she too spent many hours in the barn feeding the animals and milking the cow. The children would be left alone in the house and as usual, they had strict instructions that the older children would look after the younger ones.

It was bitterly cold. The snow was falling and winter set in with a vengeance. Metro went into the bush to cut wood. The snow became heavy and thick and the wind came up. He had worked hard most of the day. The sweat was pouring off him and he took off his coat to cool down. He had almost a full load of wood on the sleigh when the blizzard hit. He was trying to finish quickly and became hot and sweaty from working so fast. He knew he had better hurry and get home as he could easily lose his way in the blowing snow. He had to make a decision. He would either have to leave now without a full load or freeze to death if he should lose his way in the bush. He decided to leave for home immediately. It was the worst snow fall of the season and Metro knew he had better hurry. Instead of walking behind the sleigh as he normally did, he decided to climb up on top of the wood and proceeded home in the storm. He could barely see where he was going as the snow whipped about his face. He was afraid that he had already lost his sense of direction.

Metro was numb with the cold and he was losing his sense of awareness. His eyes started to close and he would try to shake himself back to reality. Metro prayed to God to let the horses find the way back to the farm house. Somehow the horses managed to find their way and eventually they stopped in front of the house. By this time, Metro had no idea where he was or how he got there. He was half frozen on top of the wood and could not get down on his own.

Anna had been worried about him when the storm hit. She spotted him the minute the team arrived in front of the house. She ran out quickly as she wondered why Metro was not making a move to ascend from the sleigh. She helped him get down and into the house. He could barely walk he was so stiff. The sweat on his body was frozen and he was trembling with the cold. Anna got Metro upstairs, stripped off his clothes and got him into bed under the feather tick. She then ran back outside to take the team of horses into the barn. She was exhausted with all the rushing around as she wondered how her husband was doing. Metro was very ill. He could barely speak he was so cold. His body was quivering and Anna decided that she would have to get the doctor as soon as the storm let up.

Anna proceeded to boil some wheat. She boiled it until it was reasonably swelled and then she let it cool down a bit. She placed the wheat into burlap bags and while it was still steaming, she lay one at

Metro's back, one around his chest and the third burlap bag filled with wheat she placed at his feet. Metro told Anna that his head hurt him. Anna placed a burlap bag of wheat at his head too. Then she covered him up with the warm feather tick and induced him to perspire.

She watched Metro very carefully that night. Eventually she fell asleep herself. The next morning when Anna awakened she stared in horror at her husband. She whipped the burlap bag off his head. She could not believe her eyes. Metro's hair had turned completely white during the night! His hair had been a beautiful red colour and just like that it was gone forever. Anna became very frightened. She knew that Metro had to be very ill indeed. The storm had subsided and she made arrangements with a neighbour to get the doctor to come and see her husband.

A doctor came down to the house in his fancy horse drawn covered sleigh a couple of days later. Upon examining Metro, he advised Anna that Metro had, at most, approximately six months to live. He had absolutely no hope for him. He advised Anna that Metro would not survive the terrible ordeal he had been put through. He also told Anna that he thought Metro had pneumonia and nothing more could be done for him.

Anna would not believe the doctor and decided that she would continue the wheat process. In the following weeks to the amazement of everyone, Metro slowly appeared to be improving. With each day he gained a little more strength. Anna was anxious and prayed a great deal.

Some days Anna would make Metro lay on his stomach and she would place a half of a raw potato on his back. Then she would insert wooden matches into the potato, usually about a half a dozen of them, and light the matches. Immediately she would place a quart jar over the entire potato. The matches would go out, smothered by the placement of the jar. The suction would draw the flesh up into the mouth of the jar and Anna would slowly ease the pressure of the suction by placing a finger at the base of the jar and releasing the air a little bit at a time. Anna would apply this to five or six places on Metro's back. This procedure, according to Anna, would draw the bad blood up to the surface and help circulate the good blood into the body. She repeated this process a couple of times a week. It left Metro with bluish red circles all over his back.

Almost daily, Anna would crush several cloves of garlic and when it was mashed into juice, she would apply the garlic to Metro's back, palms, feet and chest. This would ease the congestion in his lungs Anna said.

When Metro was strong enough to sit up, Anna decided that she would try something else. She sent one of the boys out to the pile of stones in the field and asked him to bring back a couple of large ten pound rocks, which he did. She placed the large rocks into the fire in the stove to get them hot. There was a wooden tub which had held some pickled herring in it at one time. Anna had purchased it for washing her clothes in. She filled the tub partially with cold water. When the rocks got hot, she pulled them out of the fire with a shovel and placed them into the tub of water. Then she lay a couple of flat boards across the tub and had Metro sit on the boards with a blanket pulled tightly around him and the tub. This was, in a way, a sauna bath she was giving him. She continued this process for a long time until Metro was well enough to walk by himself again. She had nursed him back to health and she amazed all her neighbours who had thought that Metro would die that winter.

Later Metro admitted that if he had walked behind the team instead of riding on top of the logs, he probably would not have been so cold. Because he was sitting still, the cold had gripped him much quicker and froze his entire sweating body. On the other hand, he speculated, because of the blowing snow, he could not have led the horses to the house. He had to let the horses find their own way home.

Meanwhile the chores still had to be done. The boys were too young to help Anna. All that winter while Metro was recuperating, Anna was left to do the chores and this placed a heavy burden on Anna and her family. She was getting heavy with child and this left quite a strain on her. By nightfall, Anna was usually exhausted. The wood still had to be chopped for their own use as well as for the school. Anna had to ask her brother to help her in that regard.

In the spring Metro was well enough to be able to go to the barn and feed the animals and help with some of the chores to ease Anna's heavy load a bit. It was very strange for Anna to see her husband and his pure white hair. He was still as handsome as he ever was and she was happy to have him alive and well.

Early that spring, Anna sent Michael to fetch the midwife. She gave birth to another child, born April 14th 1924. It was her third girl and they named her Nellie. She was a beautiful child and blonde like the others. From the start, she gained a lot of weight. She was always considered a chubby baby. She was also Metro's favourite.

The neighbours were in awe to see Metro up and about doing his chores that spring. They were also amazed to see his pure white hair and they marvelled at Anna and her healing techniques. Metro was 36 years of age.

Mowat School, Mossey River Manitoba

Chapter 9

Playing With Fire

Anna and Metro did not do the planting of the wheat that spring. Anna had put her garden in as usual though and with the help of the older boys, she managed quite well. When it was necessary, she kept them home from school to help in that regard.

Metro was getting better too. By June he was almost as good as new and back to his normal self again. His legs bothered him a bit, but he was starting to chase Anna around the barn as usual. He spent a great deal of time with Nellie, while he was improving. The two of them bonded together and developed a great love for one another. Anna was grateful for the time Metro spent with the infant as this gave her more time to attend to other matters.

The following winter was a difficult one for Anna. They did not have any wheat money to rely on. She did, however, have the granary full as usual and this was very helpful in getting them through the cold winter months. Metro had been well enough to cut the wood for the winter for their own use.

Anna was pregnant again and expecting the following spring. On March 31, 1925, Sonia was born to Anna and was her fifth daughter. The neighbours were amazed and said that they expected Anna to have another baby the following spring. They marvelled at Metro's improving health and his capabilities. Anna ignored them and went about her business as usual. Sonia was a healthy child too and blonde like the rest of the children. The family loved the little one and kissed and hugged her and all wanted to hold her.

Nellie was just over a year old and the baby fat was still showing. She seemed to gain weight on a regular basis. Anna said it was normal for the child. She was still Metro's favourite and he would spend a great deal of time singing to her when he was putting her to bed at night. He adored the little girl and she adored him too.

Later that spring Metro got out the team of horses to plough the land ready for the planting of the wheat. Anna was relieved and thanked God for his improving health.

That fall Anna was grateful for the wheat harvested, transported to the grain elevators in Fork River and sold. She had the granary well stocked too and the root cellar was full of vegetables. Things were back to normal. The children were off to school and she and Metro could get away now and again for a few hours. Michael was twelve years old going on thirteen and was a tremendous help around the farm as was Andrew.

Anna was pregnant again and expecting the following May. She and Metro were preparing to go into Fork River for some supplies. Anna had to mix the flour for the bread before she left. She hurried as she kneaded the dough and placed it in the two pans to rise. She did not use the pyatz during the winter months. This meant that she had to bake bread every day to feed the children. She fed the older children when they awakened and soon they were off to school.

It was a bitterly cold day in February. Anna and Metro were about ready to leave for the trip to Fork River. Some days Anna just felt that she had to get away from the farm, the house and the children for a few hours. She checked on her moonshine. It was working just fine and dripping into a pan. She had two gallon jugs hidden in the snow already and only she and Metro knew where they were buried.

Anna decided to keep Pauline home from school this day. She was reluctant to leave the small children alone again but she knew she could not take them with her. She instructed Pauline, who was seven years old, that she was in charge of the household while Anna was away. The older children, Michael, Andrew, Fred and Mary were at school.

Pauline was like a little mother. Anna depended on Pauline and had a great deal of faith in her. She instructed Pauline to bake the bread as soon as it had risen. She told her to put three pieces of wood on the fire, place one loaf into the oven and when it was baked, she was to do the same with the other loaf of bread.

After they had left, Pauline peeled the potatoes in readiness for supper. The smaller boys were playing upstairs and then they got hungry. They came downstairs naked as they usually were and got some potatoes out of the pot. They sliced the potatoes and placed them on top of the buck stove to bake. They had often done this and Pauline let them bake their potato slices. She commenced with the preparation of baking the first loaf of bread. She threw three pieces of wood into the stove as Anna had instructed and placed a loaf of bread in the oven.

The boys began to fight over their potatoes. Johnny said that Bill had taken his potato and eaten it and Bill claimed that Johnny had taken the potatoes from his side of the buck stove. They began wrestling on the floor beside the buck stove and knocked one of the legs out from under the burning pot-belly stove and it fell over. The pipes scattered all over the wooden floor. The red hot buck stove was lying on its side. The place started to fill up with smoke. Fortunately, the stove did not fall on top of the two boys and this thought frightened Pauline.

Pauline grabbed a pail of melted snow and poured it into the opening of the buck stove. She hoped that the fire would go out. She then gathered the boys and went upstairs where Jessie, Nellie and Sonia were. She tucked them all into bed and gave Jessie the bottle to give to the infant Sonia. Sonia was eleven months old. Pauline covered them up with the feather tick and told them to stay there unless she instructed them otherwise.

She went back downstairs and checked on the buck stove. The fire was still smothering but there appeared to be no flames. The house was full of smoke. She knew she could not open the windows as there was approximately an inch of ice on the windows. So she opened the door wide to let the smoke out of the house.

Even the dog knew something was wrong. It was very cold outside. He never came into the house but this time he sniffed at the door. Pauline quickly ran up the stairs to join the smaller children and crawled into bed with the others. She had figured on an alternate plan. She told the children that if there was a fire, they should all follow her with the feather tick to the barn where there was a hay loft and they could all sleep there. Pauline became very stressed out and started to chew her nails. She chewed them so much that they were almost bleeding. It was a great responsibility for a seven year old child to bear. Mercifully, they eventually all fell asleep.

It was late afternoon when the four children arrived home from school. They were shocked to see the door wide open and the dog sitting in the doorway. Michael knew something had happened and upon entering the house, he quickly assessed the situation. He sent the others upstairs to check on the younger children. Soon they came back downstairs and told him that the other children were all right and were fast asleep.

Michael and Andrew immediately took charge and set the buck stove back into place, arranged the pipes to it and soon had the fire restarted again. The house was very cold and the temperature outside was well below zero. Michael was thirteen years old, but he was a responsible child too. They relit the fire in the cooking stove as well and, of course, the bread was wasted and had to be thrown out. It was frozen solid just as everything else had been.

That day Pauline, although she was only seven years old, became a woman. She had grown up literally overnight. Anna could always count on Pauline for just about anything. Pauline was the second little mother in Anna's house.

When Anna and Metro returned home and found out what had happened, they were appalled. The house could have burned down.

The children could all have died from asphyxiation. They could also have frozen to death if not for Pauline. If not for her daughter, they could have all died in several different ways. Anna knelt down and thanked God again for her daughter and her wise actions that saved the lives of her younger children.

Anna had to leave her children alone many more times after that. She did not relish the thought of leaving them alone, but with so many children it had become a necessity. She had other things to do and could not always be at home watching over her children. Again, her rule applied. The older children looked after the younger ones in her household.

Anna's Father, Harry Zabiaka

Chapter 10

Gopher Tales

It had been a cold and harsh winter. After the near fire, Anna was more hesitant than ever to leave her children alone, but the chores still had to be done and the trips to Fork River were also essential.

Michael and Andrew were now in their teens. They were still playing the violin and the cymbali. They had learned new songs and Anna would listen critically while they practised their pieces. The year was 1926.

Metro was feeling better each day and was soon to his normal self again. He had planted the wheat that spring with the help of some of his good neighbours and Michael and Andrew. Anna was heavy with child and was expecting any day.

Anna got her garden started in the spring but it was not all in. She began to get labour pains and Metro was about to hitch the team and go to fetch the midwife. Anna advised him that it was too late for that. The baby was due anytime. Metro was reluctant to be by himself again but this had all happened twice before. He got the hot water and prepared himself for the birth of the baby. It was May 23, 1926. Anna gave birth to another boy. They christened him Peter. He was the sixth boy living and Anna thanked God again that he was a healthy baby boy.

Anna told the boys to help Metro get the rest of the garden in. Pretty soon she was up and about doing her chores as well. The cow was ready for breeding, Anna noted. She told Metro to contact the local farmer who had a bull and get the necessary arrangements made to breed the cow. Soon after, Metro put a rope around the cow's neck and walked her over to the farmer's place. He was gone for the better part of the day. They paid the farmer by giving him one of the pigs for having the cow serviced.

One of the children came home from school with a bad cold. Pretty soon all the children caught the cold and they all started to cough and sneeze. Anna was used to this. It happened frequently. If one of the children had a cold the rest would soon catch it too. Anna would go into her garlic storage bin, pull out the garlic cloves and mash them until it became juice. She would then apply it on their chest and on their feet. The smell of garlic would fill up the entire house. Usually the remedy worked very well.

Nellie was still considered overweight and the boys would tease her and call her "chubby." Metro would get upset with the boys and would tell them to be quiet. Nellie was still his favourite and she would run to his arms every time he came in the door. She was going on three and was a very beautiful child.

Everything was going well for them. The children were going to school. Metro was feeling much better. The older children looked after the younger ones and Anna could get away now and again to Fork River without worrying about her children.

They discussed the possibility of buying the old homestead and making it their very own permanent home. Nothing came out of their discussions though. They continued to farm the land and clearing the stones from the field.

The gopher holes were numerous in the field. It was extremely dangerous for the horses when they trod through the field. A step into one of these holes would possibly mean a broken leg for the horses.

The government had issued a bounty on the gopher tails. The boys called them "flicker tails." They would go out into the fields and pour water into one end of the gopher hole and have a snare waiting at the other end of the hole. When the gopher would stick its head out, they would yank on the string and capture the gopher around its neck. They would then step on its head and remove the tail. The animal would then be released. The boys thought that the tails would eventually grow back on the gophers. The population of the gophers would not be decreased in any event. They had been doing this for quite some time before Metro and Anna found out and straightened them up on it. The boys received quite a bit of pocket money when they brought in the flicker tails for redemption by the government.

Later the cow was ready to give birth to the calf. Anna ran across the road to fetch her brother Fred to help them. Between the three of them, they managed very well and the cow gave birth to a heifer. The children wanted to watch the cow give birth and Anna allowed them to witness the event. They were fascinated by the whole affair and later discussed it at school with the other children. Anna decided they would raise the calf and sell it the following spring.

That fall, Anna managed to get all her garden in the root cellar in readiness for the winter. The wheat too had been harvested and transported to Fork River and sold. They had sufficient money to tide them over the cold winter months.

The snow had fallen and winter was upon them. Anna had the moonshine buried in the snow. She had been selling the moonshine to some of the local farmers and they always came back for more. She was doing a thriving business with the homebrew. It was no secret that if one wanted a bottle of whisky Anna Kuzyk had it for sale.

Anna woke Metro up early this cold winter morning. He went out and brought in some firewood for the day. He also went into the barn to feed the animals. Anna would be coming shortly to milk the cow. He tarried in the barn and the warmth from the animals made him feel warm too.

Anna appeared very soon and started to milk the cow. Metro was in a loving mood and began to play up to Anna. They had very little privacy in the house because of the children. Metro was getting very playful. Anna would not have any of it and warned him that she had to get the cow milked. Metro never stopped trying and the older children were aware of some of the things that went on in the barn, but they kept quiet about it.

The following summer of 1927, just before the summer holidays the older children had gone to school as usual. They were nearing the bridge that crossed the river. There were a lot of loose planks on the bridge. The vehicles usually slowed down when crossing it. Johnny was just six years old and tried to keep up with the older boys in everything they did.

An old flat bed truck happened to come by and slowed down at the bridge just as the children were ready to cross it. Andrew, who was almost thirteen years old, jumped on the back of the truck when it slowed down and Johnny too decided to hitch a ride. As soon as the truck crossed the bridge, Andrew jumped off because it was starting to pick up speed again. Johnny went to jump off too but his coveralls caught on a nail and he was being dragged along the road as the truck speeded up and his head kept banging on the gravel road.

The children stood and looked on in horror as Johnny was being dragged along. Mercifully, the coveralls ripped and down came Johnny. It all happened so quickly and suddenly. He was lying very still on the road. He was badly bruised and semi-conscious. The older children managed to get him home. Anna was terrified when she saw her son and the condition he was in. She got some cold water from the well. She then placed cold compresses on his head and tried talking to him, asking him where he was hurting. For several days she nursed him and finally he opened his eyes but there was a strange look in them.

Anna did not have medicine to cure Johnny's ails. She had a lot of work to do and could not stay with Johnny all the time. She told Pauline to stay home from school to look after him. Pauline was frightened because Johnny was acting so strange. He seemed dazed and did not know where he was. He appeared not to know Pauline. He would get up and start to wander about the house and yard. Pauline cautiously followed him around. He would turn about and yell at her in strange way. He would scream at her to leave him alone. This frightened Pauline even more. She was truly afraid of Johnny. Pauline looked after him for a whole week. He hardly ate anything and Anna was very concerned about him.

One day Pauline made some borscht. She cautiously approached Johnny and asked him if he would like some. The glazed look in his eyes appeared to be gone and he told Pauline that he would like something to eat. He ate all the borscht with relish. He then told Pauline that he had to go and feed the chickens. He had called her by name! She agreed to let him go but followed him closely.

He got some wheat out of the bag. Then he proceeded into the yard to the chicken coop and commenced to feed the chickens. He came back to the house and seemed to know where he was. Again, he called Pauline by name. Pauline was overjoyed and told Johnny to go back to bed and rest. Somehow she knew the worst was over. She kissed him on his forehead and he went back to sleep. Pauline was nine years old.

Anna thanked God for saving her little boy. She kept him home from school for the balance of the month. The summer holidays had rolled around and Anna was grateful for that. Johnny was soon his usual self and played with the others as he normally did.

Fork River Bridge 1927

Chapter 11

Accident Prone

Pauline had been a great deal of help to Anna. She had stayed home from school for the balance of the month of June. Anna was happy for the summer holidays. At least she would not need to keep any of the children home from school during the summer months. She always felt she was robbing them of their education when she did make one of them stay at home. Anna went about her chores. She also had two houses to plaster before fall and she was away a whole lot.

Johnny would recuperate during the summer months and would be starting back to school in September. Pauline still looked after him and watched him carefully wherever he went and whatever he did. She felt responsible for him and Anna knew he was in good hands.

For some reason Anna did not rely on Mary the way she did on Pauline. Mary was two and a half years older than Pauline. Mary was good in the house with cooking, cleaning and washing clothes. Pauline was better with the children. Anna tended to favour Mary when it came to any physical labour because of her illness as a small baby.

It was the summer holidays and all the children were home from school. Anna was away plastering the houses. Mary was busy with the chores in the house and preparing the potatoes for the evening meal. Metro and Michael were in the house playing cards and looking after the smaller children. Pauline, Andrew and Fred were in the barn playing. They were all bare feet as they normally were during the hot summer months. They were enjoying themselves playing in the hay.

They would climb up into the hay loft, swing by grabbing hold of the beams in front of them and landing on the pile of hay below. They were having a great time. Suddenly Pauline jumped off, landed on the hay and felt a sharp pain in her foot. She screamed and called for the boys to help her. Fred came running over and discovered that Pauline had landed on the pitchfork. One of the prongs was embedded in Pauline's foot. Without thinking, Fred yanked the pitchfork out of her foot. Pauline looked at her foot and to her surprise, the foot did not bleed very much. They continued to play and soon Jessie joined the group.

There was an opening about a foot wide between the beams. It was just wide enough for their heads to pass through as they would swing and jump on the hay below. They continued to play when suddenly Jessie jumped and her head got caught between the two beams. Her little arms were clutching at the air for something to grab a hold of. Pauline looked on in horror as her sister hung there by her chin. Once again, she screamed for the boys. Andrew quickly climbed on top of the beams and pulled Jessie up by her armpits. It was a miracle that she did not break her neck. They were all very frightened. They decided that they had enough of the barn for one day. They went back into the house. Pauline bathed her foot in water and it seemed to look alright to her. The prong had apparently passed through it cleanly and had not severed any tendons. Later she told Anna about her accident. Anna put some salve on it and wrapped it up. Pretty soon Pauline did not feel any pain and her foot healed very quickly after that.

One day the boys were playing in the woods at the back of the house. They noticed a crow's nest high up in the tree. Reluctant to climb up themselves, the older boys asked Johnny, who was very agile, to climb up and bring down the crow's nest with the eggs in it. Johnny was still recuperating from the truck accident, but he did not want to disappoint the older boys so up the tree he climbed. He managed to get the nest separated from the tree and began to slowly descend with the eggs intact. It was very difficult to ascend with one hand being occupied with the nest and Johnny lost his balance and fell to the ground on top of a stump beside the tree. His back took the brunt of the fall and knocked the breath out of him. The older boys hurried to his side and comforted Johnny. His back was sore he said, but otherwise he appeared not to be hurt. The older boys warned Johnny not to say anything to Anna as she would be very upset. So Johnny promised not to tell his mother about his fall. The crow's nest, of course, had fallen apart and the eggs had been broken. The entire exercise was for naught.

Johnny would get into more trouble. The well which was about 25 feet deep had suddenly dried up. Johnny, on his own, took it upon himself to investigate. He climbed into the bucket which of course then went straight to the bottom with him in it. He was knocked unconscious for quite some time. When he came to, he hollered for help and luckily the others heard him. They told him to get back into the bucket and they cranked the bucket up and got him out. Other than a few bumps and bruises, he sustained no other injuries.

It was a very busy time for Anna. She was still working on the two houses she had to plaster. Anna also had the vegetables to dig up and store in the root cellar before winter set in.

Metro and the boys had the wheat to get harvested and Anna together with the smaller children looked after the garden. Everyone did their fair share of the work around harvest time. Anna did what she could and left the balance of the vegetables for the children and Metro to get in. She had to go away again.

She still worried about Johnny at times. He seemed to be normal, although there were times when she would detect a strange behaviour about him. He did not appear to be as active as he used to be.

Metro had a contract with the school to provide them with wood for the winter months and he was away a lot in the bush cutting wood. He wanted to get as much done as possible before the cold weather set in.

Anna had just about finished the two houses she was plastering and Metro thanked God for that. She had been away so much the past summer and worked so hard. He was beginning to resent her absence and the fact that he was left to do all the chores alone too.

The wheat had been threshed. The garden was in the root cellar and Anna managed to get all the cucumbers picked and pickled. The cucumbers were in the granary soaking in brine. Somehow things managed to get done and winter was soon upon them.

Anna was different after the birth of Peter. She did not get pregnant again for a couple of years. It was the longest period between pregnancies since her marriage to Metro. Late the following fall Anna did become pregnant again. She was not showing yet and she was happy about that. She was also very careful about walking outside the house during the winter months. She avoided the ice whenever she went to do her chores.

Anna was just relaxing and stemming her feathers one evening beside the stove. She was listening to Metro as he read her the love story about a young soldier and his sweetheart. Anna shook her head from side to side as she listened. Her eyes filled with tears and Metro did not notice as he continued with the story.

The children's' underwear was hanging on a clothes line in the house. The long johns were brought in from outside and they were frozen solid. The children were running around naked as usual just before bedtime. They all needed to go to the toilet first and would run outside without any clothes on and take turns using the toilet. Anna continued to shake her head as she listened to the story Metro was relating.

The winter had not been too bad for the family. There was plenty to eat and Metro made some money chopping wood. Anna too had some money put away from the plastering of the houses. She also made a few dollars selling the moonshine to the local farmers. All in all it was an average winter.

The following spring they once more got their wheat and garden in and Anna was heavy with child. She kept Pauline home quite often to help her watch the children while Anna did her chores. She was grateful for the summer holidays again, because then the children were home from school and were a tremendous help around the house.

It was a hot and muggy day in August, 1929, the year and month of the stock market crash that Anna gave birth to a baby girl. Her sixth daughter was born on August 25 and they named her Stella. She, like the others, was a healthy baby and Anna, as always, thanked God. Everyone rallied around the child and fought to hold her. They always loved the youngest and would kiss and admire the infants. They were a loving family. Nellie especially was attentive to Stella and would kiss her goodnight every night. Metro would lift her up to the hanging cradle over the bed and let her give Stella a goodnight kiss.

Metro approached Anna one day and expressed his concerns about Nellie. Nellie was not feeling very well. She was hot and feverish of late. She was also listless and not very hungry. She complained about being tired all the time. Sometimes Nellie would wander around aimlessly and whimper as she went along. This was very unusual for her and Metro thought that they should call the doctor to examine her.

The doctor arrived and diagnosed Nellie as having diphtheria. She had a high fever and was very weak. It was a highly contagious disease he said and he was afraid for the other children in the house. He gave Nellie a shot in the throat and said he would stop by in another week to administer another shot. He would arrive on schedule once a week, examine the child and give her the usual shot. Nellie was petrified of the man and screamed in terror every time he arrived. It broke Metro's heart to see her so frightened and he could do nothing to ease her anxiety.

This went on for about a month. The doctor came by this one day and gave Nellie her usual shot and left the house. It was the end of October and it was a cold night. Nellie asked Metro to lift her up to the cradle and let her kiss Stella goodnight. He lifted her up and she said her goodnight. Then she lay down beside Anna. Metro put out the lights and started to go to bed too. He heard Nellie cry out. He quickly put the lights back on and picked the child up. She defecated in his arms and died. Nellie passed away on October 31, 1929 at the age of five. It was sadly, on Metro's 42 birthday.

Anna and Metro were heartbroken. Metro wept unashamedly while he held the little one. The others cried too and the boys felt remorseful for being mean to Nellie and calling her chubby. Anna prayed to God and sat on the bed. She rocked herself slowly back and forth as the tears streamed down her face.

They buried the little girl in a cemetery not far from the school and the children would always stop by on their way to the school and say hello to their baby sister. Anna forbade any music in the house during the mourning period. She considered it disrespectful. They all mourned Nellie for a long time to come.

Hauling Wood, Mossey River 1928

Chapter 12

Tarred and Feathered

A week later Anna got up very early. It was a cold November morning. Winter was fast approaching and there was still a lot to be done before winter set in. She woke Metro who went out and brought in some wood for the fire which Anna had already started in the stove. He then proceeded to the barn to feed the animals. He was still feeling sad and the death of his little girl had really affected him.

Anna went into the barn to milk the cow and when she spotted Metro her heart went out to him. For the past week he did not make any moves toward her and she knew he was not his usual self. She set her pail down and walked over to him. She put her arms around him and tried to comfort him. He sighed and put his arms around Anna and together they held each other for a while. She wanted so much to make his sorrow go away. They consoled each other and Metro was grateful to Anna for her rare moment of tenderness.

Later Anna milked her cow and returned to the house. Metro told Anna that he wanted to stay in the barn for a while. He cried softly and was slowly unwinding. Only the animals in the barn could hear him and it was somehow, very comforting. He remained in the barn for quite some time.

It was Saturday and they had to go into Fork River for some supplies before the snow fell. Anna had to bake bread in the pyatz for the children before they departed. She knew Metro needed this time for himself however, and she did not want to rush him. It was about an hour and half journey by wagon into town. She kneaded the dough and left it to rest. She had to bake the bread every other day as it was the main staple food for the children. Usually she baked about twelve loaves at one time. It was a lot of dough to knead.

Then she prepared the cream in two quart jars and told the boys to start shaking them to make butter. She usually left Mary in charge of the household on weekends and told her to do the laundry while they were away. Mary fetched two pails of water from the well and set them on the stove to heat.

By nine o'clock the bread was baking in the outdoor oven. Metro came back from the barn feeling much better and they prepared for their departure.

It was a beautiful sunny day but it was windy. The leaves had changed colour, had fallen and were swirling around in the front yard. Anna was pleased with the way things had progressed as far as the crops were concerned.

The wheat had been threshed, harvested and transported to one of the two grain elevators in Fork River. Her brother and the older boys had helped with the harvest and it was a good one. Anna felt they received a fair price for the wheat. The money would be sufficient to tide them over the winter months. The garden had been very productive too. The root cellar was full with plenty of potatoes, carrots, beets and cabbage.

The granary was also well stocked. The children had been instrumental in the picking of the cranberries. Anna had made cranberry jam and it was stored in two ten gallon crocks, covered with a linen cloth in the granary. A ten gallon crock of sauerkraut was also stored in the granary.

Anna made dill pickles in a large wooden barrel. The pickles were covered with brine and a clean rock was placed on top of a cutting board to hold down the pickles. She also had a few sacks of feathers stored in the granary for her winter project. There was always a shortage of feather ticks and pillows in the house.

They set off about noon. The bread was baked, the butter was made and the children were fed. The children did not bother to cut the bread but merely broke the crusty bread up into pieces while it was still warm, put freshly made butter on it and washed it all down with the buttermilk.

Anna took the balance of the butter, placed it in the pail and lowered it into the well. She always kept her butter in the well to keep it from melting during the hot summer months. It was cooler in the water and preserved the butter. Anna left strict instructions for the boys to feed the pigs in the late afternoon, in case Metro and she were detained for some reason.

Upon their arrival at Fork River, they met other neighbours who, like them, were in town to pick up last minute supplies before the snow fell. They each chatted with other people and Metro took a few minutes to sneak a "roll your own" cigarette from one of the men, being careful so that Anna would not see him. She was adamant about his not smoking. Occasionally, he would ask a neighbour for a cigarette when Anna was not looking. They all extended their sympathies about the baby daughter Anna and Metro had just buried and Metro's eyes filled up with tears as he thought about his little girl.

After they had made their purchases of several 50 pound bags of flour, a 50 pound bag of sugar, some kerosene for the coal oil lamps, salt, matches and numerous other items, it was time to head for home. They loaded the wagon and set out on the trip back. Anna was quite anxious to get home as it got dark fairly early. The wind was still brisk and as they rode through the area of the bush, the trees cast shadows and played tricks on Anna. She shivered more from anxiety than the cold.

It was dusk as they neared the front yard. Anna could see the faint light of the coal oil lamp glowing through the window in the house and it cast an eerie spell over her. Something was not right. She felt a sense of foreboding. As her eyes became accustomed to the surroundings, a bizarre sight greeted them. There appeared to be strange creatures scurrying about the yard chasing the swirling leaves. It was something like she had never seen before in her life! Anna's heart throbbed rapidly in her chest and she screamed in terror!

"My God, my God, Metro what in heavens name is that?" She cried out hysterically. The horses reared in fright and Metro had some trouble in controlling the team. Anna lost her balance and nearly fell off the wagon. "Its the pigs, Anna, its the pigs." Metro yelled back as he assessed the situation and brought the horses to a halt. Anna was terrified but eventually calmed down a little. She began to take in the scene around her. She noticed that the granary door was flung wide open and on further investigation at the house, she found that the boys had apparently fed the pigs but did not close the pig pen. The boys had also been into the granary for some pickles and had left the door of the granary open. The pigs got out of the pen, entered the granary and subsequently got into the cranberry jam and the feathers Anna had stored. The pigs were literally tarred with jam and feathered. Anna was devastated. Needless to say, there was no cranberry jam for anyone that winter.

Anna's Barn

Chapter 13

Young Love

Mary was fourteen years of age. She decided that it was going to be her last year at school. The children attended at the Mowat School and they were having their Christmas plays. The neighbouring school attended as they usually did at that time of year, to view each other's performances. They would alternate and attend at the North Lake school the following day to see their plays.

Mary spotted the young man immediately. He was attending the North Lake School. She had not noticed him before and he was so handsome she thought. His name was Steve Toporowski and Mary was in love. He showed some interest in her as well but nothing developed out of that meeting. Michael and the Toporowski lad eventually became good friends and were constantly together. The Toporowski lad would come and visit Michael and would try and break the ice with Mary. Anna noticed this and cautioned her daughter about being alone with him.

The following summer Mary discussed with Anna the fact that she would not be going back to school in September. She wanted to get a job just like her friend. Mary's friend had advised her that she would be going to Flin Flon where she knew some rich people who owned a bakery. She advised Mary that she would be getting a job in Flin Flon and staying there for the balance of the summer. It sounded very glamorous to Mary and she thought that she might go to Flin Flon and get a job there too. She discussed it with Anna and Anna agreed reluctantly to let Mary go.

Metro and Anna drove Mary to the train depot in Fork River and Anna was very sad to see her first daughter going away by herself. She was very young and Anna worried about her. Mary arrived in Flin Flon and went to the bakery to see about her friend. A discussion ensued with the owner about her looking for a job and would he know of anyone who she could work for. Immediately, the owner suggested that his wife needed a live-in housekeeper and would Mary be interested in that type of work. Mary agreed and so it was that she began to work for Mrs. Flocks. Her friend from Fork River was also working and they would meet quite often and spend at great deal of time together. Mary was very happy with the new job.

Meanwhile back home the Toporowski lad wondered about Mary. One day he asked Michael where she was. Michael advised him that she was in Flin Flon working. When he found out about this, he asked Michael for her address so that he could write to her. Michael gave him the address and the young man commenced writing to Mary. Mary was very happy to receive a letter from the man of her dreams. She started to write to him too. Their letters soon became quite serious. They wrote frequently and Anna was made aware of this situation. Mary wrote home quite often as well. She enjoyed the housekeeping duties and Mrs. Flocks liked Mary very much. Mary worked hard and long hours. She had one day off every week to do whatever she wished and Mary chose this time to spend with her friend from Fork River. She saved her money and felt very important. Her friend from Fork River was seeing a young man as well. She had met him at a gathering and he was getting very serious about her too. They were discussing marriage and Mary was very happy for her friend.

Meanwhile back on the farm Anna was occupied with the usual chores. She had a house to plaster and this kept her busy. Metro was feeling better and was out chopping wood. He was not as strong as he once was but he could still chop wood and tend to the animals in the barn.

In the spring Metro took the cow to the farmer's place again and returned in the late afternoon. They had two cows now and Anna had been busy milking both of them. Later, the cow delivered a calf and it was a male heifer. Anna and Metro had spent long hours in the barn waiting for the birth of the calf. It happened in the wee hours of the morning. Both were exhausted but were happy that the animal was healthy and strong. They eventually sold two of the cows when the calf was weaned. Anna was pleased with the money they made on them.

Anna made her own cottage cheese. She would also separate the milk from the cream and sell the cream to the local neighbours. Sometimes she would take it into Fork River and barter it for some of the supplies she and Metro needed for the farm.

Anna also raised her own pigs. She had a sow and a boar and they had ten piglets. When they were weaned, she would separate them, fatten them up and sell off the young pigs, keeping the sow and the boar.

The chickens were multiplying as well. She had several brood hens sitting on at least a dozen eggs apiece. She also used eggs for bartering. She would gather the eggs on a daily basis until she had sufficient to take to Fork River and sell at one of the general stores.

Anna made butter to sell at the general store in Fork River as well. The children would help her by shaking the jars until the butter was made. Sometimes Anna would borrow the butter churn from a neighbour if she had a lot of butter to make. The children would then fight over who would have the buttermilk.

Everything was going well for them. Anna had her garden in and Metro had planted the wheat in the spring with the assistance of the older boys. Anna would proudly give away some of her vegetables. Her cabbage was heavy and big and the neighbours would comment on what a beautiful garden Anna had. She was very generous and it made her feel good to give what she had to someone who was not as fortunate. She would often say that she did not have too much to give but if someone came to her door hungry, she would always share her food with the needy and would never turn anyone away.

Anna Feeding Her Chickens

Chapter 14

Hours of Agony

That fall Metro, with the help of the two older boys, got the wheat harvested and transported to the grain elevator in Fork River. Anna went with him to make sure they got a good price for the wheat. The garden was harvested as well and all the vegetables were taken into the root cellar. The children had once again picked the cranberries for Anna's cranberry jam and this was sitting in the granary. Anna hung her garlic and onions in a dry place upstairs where the sun could get at them and left them to dry out. She needed the garlic and onions as she used the vegetables in all her cooking as well as for medicinal purposes.

Mary's friend and the young man she had met were now talking about marriage. She would become Mrs. Broschuk soon, she proudly announced to Mary. Mary continued to work for the Flocks and writing to her boyfriend.

Anna was eight months pregnant with her baby and it was Christmas. She had prepared the usual Christmas meal and they had settled down to celebrate the festive season. The children sang Christmas carols and the family was warm and cosy on this wonderful holiday.

Metro and Anna had numerous discussions for quite some time now about purchasing the old homestead. They were contemplating on buying the homestead, but nothing ever came out of their talks. Anna had saved a few dollars from plastering houses and it could be used as a down payment on the house and farm she would point out, but Metro always found some excuse to change the subject. The homestead had been good to them through the years. Most of the rocks and stones had been cleared from the field. The harvesting had been very good too. It had yielded them a great deal of wheat and the bush nearby had also provided them with ample firewood. All in all it was a good farm and perhaps they should consider buying the homestead. Anna insisted that they do something about the farm as soon as possible, but again Metro put it off for some reason.

It was a cold day in January, 1931. Anna was having labour pains. Metro hitched up the sleigh and departed to the midwife's place. Anna had been different this time and he was very worried. When the midwife arrived, Anna was standing up and in terrible agony. The midwife examined her and was worried too. She thought the child was breach. She was very concerned as she had not encountered this type of pregnancy before.

For 48 hours Anna moaned and pushed and nothing happened. Finally in desperation, Anna told the midwife that she would have to stand up. She got up and braced herself against the table with her legs wide apart and pushed. She was weak and exhausted. She prayed to God that the baby would come and it finally did. It was a baby girl, her seventh and would be her final child. It was January 28, 1931. Later they christened her Anne after Anna because she had so much pain with the child. Anna was almost 43 years old.

It had been a harsh and cold winter. The children would cut the burlap bags into squares and use it to wrap around their feet to keep them warm during their long trek to school. During some of the colder days, Anna would get Metro to hitch up the team and go and meet the children on their way back home from school. Usually the children would be overjoyed to see the sleigh because sometimes the snow would be heavy and blowing and it was near blizzard conditions. The children went to school and Anna and Metro went to Fork River to get their supplies and did their usual visiting. Mary's friend was now married and she and her husband Mr. Broschuk returned to Fork River to be with her family. Mary was still in Flin Flon and her boyfriend wanted her to come home at Easter time for a visit. They had not seen each other for quite some time now and he was getting impatient.

Suddenly, there was a knock on the door. When Anna answered it she found Mary's friend, and her new husband standing there. She invited them in and they both commented on what a nice house Anna and her family had. They also asked if they could see the rest of the place. Anna proudly showed it off and took them through the entire house. They wanted to see what the nice barn and outbuildings were like as well. Anna obliged them and again was very proud of the farm. She invited them to partake in the Christmas meal with them and they did and shortly thereafter they left. Anna thought nothing more about the visit.

A couple of weeks later, Anna had been doing some cross-stitching on a blouse she had been making. She had come to the end of the thread on the needle and had left the material on the table while she attended to other matters. Peter was just five years old. He crawled up on the bench and commenced playing with the material on the table. He was naked and bare foot even though it was cold outside. He knocked the needle on the floor and then jumped off the bench. He started to scream with pain. Anna came running to him and tried to ask him what was the matter. He told her that his foot hurt him and he could not stand on it. Anna examined his foot and to her horror she saw the needle embedded in his foot completely and she could not get it out. Peter kept saying that the bad old uncle made him a boo boo. Metro rushed over to the neighbour's place and arranged to have Peter taken to the hospital. Anna was afraid to try her hand at getting the needle out. She reasoned that the needle might travel and get to his heart and this thought frightened her. Leaving Pauline in charge, Anna and Metro took Peter to Dauphin. The doctor removed the needle and they soon brought Peter back home. Anna was very careful about leaving the needle lying around after that.

That spring Anna and Metro were making preparations to plant the wheat and garden. It was Saturday and they chose to go into Fork River for some supplies for the planting season. It was April and the snow had just started to melt.

Anna and Metro with Jessie, Sonia, Stella and Anne

Chapter 15

Moonshine Caper

Mary received a letter from her boyfriend. He wanted her to come home for a vacation. He was very serious about Mary and wanted her to come home so that he could ask her a very important question, he said. The long distance relationship was very stressful on the young man. It was summer again and Mary was lonely and homesick for the family too. She asked Mrs. Flocks to let her have a summer holiday and Mrs. Flocks consented with much reserve. So Mary packed her belongings and returned home for a summer vacation. Everyone was happy to see her. The Toporowski lad and Mary saw a great deal of each other and they both fell in love. Anna thought that Mary was still too young to be married but she did not object when the family got together to discuss the matter.

One night Anna decided to have a gathering at the house. She would invite a group of young people and have a sort of betrothal party for Mary. The boys could play their musical instruments, Anna would prepare some food and they could have a nice time. The boys and Mary agreed and were very excited about the big party they would be having.

There was excitement in the air on this fabulous summer day. It was Saturday, and the boys were getting ready for the big party. Andrew and Michael were practising their pieces. Anna, although busy, could not resist tapping her foot to the music. It was a beautiful sunny day and they expected to have a good time that evening.

Metro was feeling much better as he went about his chores. The floor had been freshly scrubbed. The house smelt fresh and clean and Anna was very proud of herself and her home. Anna thought that they just might have a little dance. The room was spacious enough to accommodate a large group. Anna had prepared some food for the evening to serve to her young guests. She busied herself and she hummed along with the boys as they played their pieces. The young people began to arrive shortly after the supper hour. The ladies would go upstairs where Anna hung a mirror, to apply face powder and to pinch their cheeks to make them rosy.

Some of the older boys asked Anna if she had any moonshine for sale. Anna obliged them and pretty soon they began to ask the girls to dance as Michael and Andrew played the first tune "Heel, Toe, And Away We Go". Anna smiled as she watched her boys play and again she was very proud.

Anna sold some moonshine and she made a few dollars. She was quite pleased with the outcome of the evening. The young people enjoyed themselves. No one drank too much and the ladies in particular thought it was a very enjoyable evening. Michael and Andrew also improved their music and self confidence with each song they played. Mary and her fiancé danced and stayed close together throughout the entire evening. Mary was due back in Flin Flon a couple of days later.

It was about a week later, Mary was gone and things were back to normal. There was a knock on the door. Jessie answered and was taken aback. She was about ten years old but knew full well who was standing at the other end of the stoop. Metro and Anna were working in the field with the older boys and, therefore, were not in the house. Two big Mounties were standing there looking down at Jessie. They asked her if they could come in and they did.

The evidence was obvious. The copper piping was still intact and, in fact, the moonshine operation was in progress. The brew was slowly dripping into a pan. They went out and arrested Metro on the spot. They took him to the Dauphin jail, taking the evidence with them. It was obvious to Anna that someone at the Saturday night gathering had gone to the police and informed them of the moonshine.

At first Anna became confused and had a panic attack. She told herself to calm down. She reasoned that the planting had been completed and the garden was in. Still, she needed Metro and could not manage the farm without him. She rocked Anne in her cradle that night, a plan was shaping up in her mind.

The next morning Anna sent Fred over to the neighbour's place with some instructions. Shortly, Fred returned with Nick Belza in his fancy car. He was one of the few neighbours who owned an automobile. Anna left Michael and Andrew at home to tend to the animals and to milk the cow. She took the other eight children with her and they all piled into the car. They sat in each other's laps and Anna had to caution them to behave. Nick Belza drove them the twenty miles into the town of Dauphin where Anna and the children got out and started to walk. As they neared the jail house, Anna instructed Fred as to what he must tell the police.

When they arrived at the jail, Fred told the Mounties that they had walked all the way from the farm to Dauphin. The police were amazed. By this time it was nearly noon and they gathered together on the steps of the building and told the police that they were hungry. Anna, with what little English she spoke, said to one of the Mounties that she "want some look at my husband". They let her see Metro and Anna explained to him what her plan was.

At noon the Mounties took the whole brood down to the restaurant for some soup and sandwiches. What an experience that was for all of them. They had never been to a restaurant before and ate everything in sight. After lunch, they once again gathered on the steps of the jail to wait.

It was a hot afternoon but Anna stuck to her plan and remained sitting on the steps. About three o'clock, one of the Mounties brought out a couple of loaves of bread and asked Fred if he wanted some bread. The loaves were devoured in a flash. They brought out some water as well because everyone was thirsty.

It was getting near the supper hour and once again the children were complaining that they were hungry. Again, they were all escorted to the restaurant for something to eat and when they got back to the jail, Anna asked the children to tell the Mounties that they were tired and needed a place to sleep. There was a long drawn out discussion in progress. It continued for some time among the police. Finally it was agreed that Anna and the children should be taken inside the jail and housed for the night.

The boys were in their glory. They had the run of the place and were very loud and boisterous. None of the children had ever seen an inside toilet and Johnny, became intrigued with it. He kept throwing the toilet paper into the bowl and flushing it again and again. It became plugged up and the water overflowed all over the jail house floor. They almost had a flood. Finally the police managed to get everyone into their bunks and to sleep.

The following morning it was to the restaurant again for breakfast. Then the police advised Anna that they would take her and the children back to the farm. Anna was very stubborn and refused to go. They promised her that something would be done for Metro if she could just be patient. Anna finally agreed and they drove the children and Anna home. Seven days later, Metro was released from jail and was back on the farm. All the charges were dropped.

Anna still made the odd bit of moonshine but it was not for sale. She was not making it on such a large scale either. In case of unexpected company, she did not have any copper piping as evidence. The moonshine was strictly for medicinal purposes only.

A newspaper reporter from Dauphin came by later to take a picture of Anna and all the children for publishing in the local newspaper.

STRANDED FORK RIVER FAMILY

Mrs. Annie Kuzak and eleven children, who walked two days to get from their home in Fork River, to Dauphin, where the husband and father, Metro Kuzak, had been jailed on a seven months' sentence under the Excise act. The family, to call attention to their destitute condition, planted themselves on the steps of the Dauphin jail. They declared Fork River authorities refused help. Temporary relief was provided by Dauphin, and the family motored back home. Metro Kuzak is still in the cells, but a movement for mitigation of his sentence is under way.

Winnipeg Press, April 1931

Chapter 16

Evicted

It was spring 1932 and Anna and Metro left for Fork River. Pauline had been left in charge of the other children. It was a lovely day and Pauline was surprised to see Mr. and Mrs. Broschuk arrive at the door. Mrs. Broschuk said she wanted to check on the farm house to see if everything was in order. She pushed her way past Pauline and into the house she came. Pauline asked her what she was doing and Mrs. Broschuk advised Pauline that the property was now hers and that the family would have to be moving very soon. They also took a walk through the out buildings. They thoroughly checked everything. Pauline was in a state of shock. She was thirteen years of age but knew full well the severity of the problem. When Anna and Metro arrived home from Fork River, Pauline explained to Anna what had transpired between Mrs. Broschuk and herself. Anna and Metro were in a state of shock too. They decided to go and visit the woman.

Mrs. Broschuk confirmed that she had indeed purchased the homestead and that Anna and her family would have to move out within a couple of weeks. She and her husband wanted to get into the house before the planting season. Anna was almost in tears. She told the woman that they had no place to go and what would they do with all the small children without a place to live in. The woman looked long and hard at Anna and told her that it was Anna's problem, because she did not make her those little babies. The baby Anne was just over a year old.

Anna and Metro had to act quickly. They had no time to waste. They went into town to see the local MPP, Mr. Ogryzlo. He was very sympathetic about their predicament. He was aware of their situation but there was nothing he could do. The farm was sold to the Broschuk's and it was now their farm. He advised them of a piece of property about 3 miles away. It had no house or other buildings, but it was closer to Fork River and it also had two gravel pits. They were told the property was for sale for the sum of $300.00 back taxes. He also advised them that he had been selling the gravel to a contractor and they should consider that aspect of the farm. It could bring them quite a bit of money. One of the gravel pits was fine sand and the other pit was very fine gravel. Anna and Metro decided to go and view the property in question.

They picked out a building spot for the house near a stream. It was very wooded and would require a lot of work clearing the bush from the area. Anna insisted that the logs cleared could be used to build the new house. Anna talked Metro into buying the property as she was desperate now. Where would they live Metro had asked. Anna explained to Metro her plan and they proceeded to Fork River to make the necessary arrangements to purchase the farm. They went back to see Mr. Ogryzlo, the MPP and purchased the property immediately. Anna had some money saved up from plastering houses and this was a good down payment on the farm.

That evening Metro, Michael, Andrew and Fred hitched up the team of horses and proceeded to dismantle the large granary on the homestead. Log by log they took it apart and drove it to the new property. There was a small knoll across from the area they choose for the farm house and this is where they unloaded the logs from the granary. They worked all through the night until all the logs had been removed. They took the floor apart and brought all the lumber down to the new site. The next day they started to put the granary back together again. They worked long and hard and put an extra floor onto the building for an upstairs as they needed the room for the children to sleep. They were tired to the point of exhaustion.

Anna explained to Metro that this was only a temporary measure until they built the house. They had to raise the roof up to accommodate an additional floor. They spent long hours putting up the building and soon had the structure completed. There were no stairs to access the second floor. The children would have to use a ladder to get to the upper area of the old granary through an opening left just for this purpose.

They then proceeded to move the furniture into the granary. It was very crowded but Anna did not mind this as long as they had a roof over their heads. It was starting to get warm outside and this certainly was in their favour.

The animals were boarded at a neighbour's farm until they could build a barn for them. When the time came for them to be out of the old homestead, Anna and her family had everything organized.

Mrs. Broschuk was furious when she discovered the granary gone and accused Anna of stealing it. Anna told her to prove that their new little log house was her granary. They had cut down the logs from their new farm and had built the small house, Anna insisted. Mrs. Broschuk decided not to press the matter any further and settled for the farm.

Mary's boyfriend wrote again and asked Mary to come down for Easter holidays. Mary decided that she would do just that. She arrived from Flin Flon and the Toporowski lad and she talked about a wedding date. Anna was very watchful. She liked the young man and knew his family. She decided that they were a good match after all. They agreed on a date, October 30, 1932. Mary never did go back to Flin Flon to work for Mrs. Flocks again.

Mary was very surprised with the outcome of the old homestead. She was extremely upset with her old friend Mrs. Broschuk. The granary was not very large but they managed to accommodate everyone, including Mary. Anna did most of her cooking outside in an open fire and coped quite well with the arrangements.

Metro and the boys immediately began to clear the bush by the stream. They hired a carpenter to come and help with the building of the new house. There were no excavations to be made except for the root cellar. Anna's brother helped as well and she was grateful to him for his assistance. They soon had the log house completed sufficiently to move into it. The structure was very similar to the previous house. There were no room dividers just two floors, one room upstairs and one room downstairs. They soon moved the furniture from the granary to the new house. There was no time to complete the interior of the house and they were content to have the big house to move around in after the crowded granary.

The boys also managed to plough up a small plot for Anna's garden and she got her garden in as soon as possible. Anna was mostly concerned about her potatoes and these she soon had planted and was very pleased with their new farm. It was their very own place and no one could buy the farm from under them again. Anna felt a sense of security about the whole thing.

Next, they proceeded to build the barn. When it was completed, they retrieved the animals from the neighbours and Metro was very pleased about his new barn. They had accomplished so much in three months. He was very tired but content.

Anna was more than happy with her new house. They had some vegetables in the root cellar from the previous house to tide them over. Pretty soon things were running as smoothly as ever and Metro and Anna settled down to life as usual. There was no land to plough or wheat to sow, but Metro did not mind this so much. There was plenty of bush to chop wood and this was his main concern.

Anna again built her pyatz diagonally across from the house. It was a big pyatz, bigger than the previous one and again, it was a labour of love for Anna. The place would not be complete without her outdoor oven.

One morning Mrs. Broschuk came over to see Anna. She was very angry and almost in tears. Her voice was trembling as she spoke. She told Anna that her boys had come down during the night and had pulled out all her vegetables out of her garden. Nothing could be salvaged she told Anna. Anna was stunned, but she had no idea what the woman was talking about. Anna was horrified. She knew how hard she had worked to get her own garden in and felt in complete sympathy with the woman in spite of what she had done to her. She told Mrs. Broschuk so and insisted that her boys did nothing of the sort. She asked the boys and they said they were home all night and knew nothing about her garden being ruined. Mrs. Broschuk pressed charges and Anna was awarded damages at trial for false accusation. Many years later after the boys were grown, Michael and Andrew confessed to destroying the garden. Anna was horrified and although it happened so long ago, she was still very saddened.

Anna's father had been ailing for quite some time now. Even before they had moved. Anna would go down to see him as often as she could but it was quite a bit further to go now and she could not just pop over whenever she wanted to.

One evening just at dusk, the dog started to howl. Everyone went outside and wondered what was the matter with the animal. Anna said that a dog usually howled like that when someone close to the family had died. She sent one of the boys over to her brother's place to inquire of her father. Everyone was amazed. Sure enough, Anna's father had passed away that evening. It was 1932 and he was 87 years old.

He was well liked in the community and everyone came down to her brother's place to pay their last respects. The priest came down and administered the last rights. They buried Anna's father in the local cemetery. On the day of the funeral there was a huge deluge of rain. The grave filled with water and all watched in horror as the coffin began floating to the surface. This was not a good omen Anna thought to herself. He had lived a full and satisfactory life and Anna could see no point in mourning the old man. What he needed now was prayers and she prayed for him.

Anna and Metro with Nine Children

Chapter 17

The Scalding

Everyone had settled in nicely into their new house and the preparations for the coming wedding in October were being made. Arrangements were under way as to the cooking of the meals. Anna and Metro decided that the wedding should be held in their new house. The house was certainly big enough. They would have to borrow some dishes and pots and pans but they had a lot of good neighbours who were willing to help out. The boys could also play their musical instruments and they could have a dance as well.

Anna worked hard on completing the feather tick and pillows for Mary's wedding present and everything was packed away in the closet upstairs ready for the wedding day.

All their friends looked forward to the wedding too. Anna took Mary into Dauphin to purchase the material for her wedding gown. Mary was just sixteen going on seventeen. They took the material over to Mrs. Hudyk's place to make the wedding gown for Mary. Mrs. Hudyk had a sewing machine and was quite adept as a seamstress. It would not be the usual traditional Ukrainian wedding garb, but Anna reasoned, they were now in Canada and things change.

All the wedding preparations were in order. Metro built a lean to beside the house. He moved the cooking stove into it to make it like a summer kitchen in readiness for the women who would be doing the cooking for the wedding. An opening was made into the main house to pass the food from the makeshift kitchen to the house.

The pipes ran through the ceiling upstairs to keep the upper portion of the house warm. When the stove was removed, so were the pipes and Metro also removed the galvanized steel plate around the pipes on the upper floor. They still had the buck stove in the centre of the house to keep them warm.

It was a cold Saturday in October 1932. The snow had not fallen but the skies were overcast and threatening. There was excitement and anticipation everywhere. It was to be a big wedding. Mary and her husband-to-be had to be driven in a car to Fishing River where the wedding ceremony took place. They were then driven back to the farm in preparation for the reception.

The neighbours and friends began to arrive. The priest was also invited to attend the reception. There were cabbage rolls, pork sausages, perogies, fried sauerkraut with sliced kielbasa, cakes and plenty of meat. Metro had killed quite a few chickens and they had plenty of roast chicken. A pig had also been slaughtered in honour of the wedding. Anna had made some moonshine in readiness for the big event as well.

The guests ate and drank and everyone was enjoying themselves. They soon filled the entire house. Later a large plate was placed in front of the bride and groom and the guests would line up and present them with money by placing it in the large plate. The best man would offer each and every guest a shot of moonshine to toast the happy couple with. Anna and Metro would be the first in line and Anna sang songs to the happy couple as she presented her money into the plate. The others soon followed suit. Mary looked beautiful in her white gown. Anna placed a sprig of fern in her veil as was the custom in the old country. The boys played their musical instruments and everyone danced until all hours of the morning.

Everything had gone well and Mary was married. The next day the wedding guests were invited to the Toporowski's place for another meal. Their weddings usually lasted three days and this too was a custom from the old country.

Metro had replaced the wood stove back in the main house and installed the pipes again. He had not, however, replaced the galvanized steel plate around the pipes in the ceiling.

The following day, Monday, Anna and Metro went to Fork River. The snow was falling and showed no signs of stopping. It had turned bitterly cold outside. They needed some more supplies as the wedding had cleaned them right out of flour and sugar. They also needed some boots for the children to go to school with. With all the preparations for the wedding, there was no time to go and buy the boots in readiness for the winter.

They left Pauline in charge of the family. Michael, Andrew and Fred were no longer going to school and were away chopping wood. Anna had kept the other children home from school. They were upstairs playing with the younger children.

Pauline was told to do the laundry. She went outside and scooped up some snow with the two pails and set them on the hot stove to melt for her washing. When she had sufficient water in the tub, she began to scrub the sheets. She had brought in two more pails of snow and they were now sitting on the stove melting and getting hot.

She had finished washing the sheets and set out to put them outside to dry. There was an old existing wooden fence running along side of the house and this was used instead of a clothes line to dry the sheets. The warm sheets were starting to freeze up in the cold. She quickly spread them open over the fence as fast as she could before they froze and cracked. She was hurrying as it was freezing and she wanted to get back into the house.

Jessie came running outside screaming for Pauline to hurry because Anne had fallen on top of the stove. Pauline's heart skipped a beat and she without thinking, grabbed the last sheet she was spreading and dashed with it into the house. Anne was indeed on the stove. She had fallen through the opening upstairs, fell along the pipes and her tiny hip lay in one pail of hot water. She had placed her small hand on the hot stove for support and it immediately blistered. Anne was just a year and 9 months old. Pauline grabbed Anne out of the water and ripped her clothes off her. She then had the presence of mind to snatch the butter off the table and spread it all over Anne. She then wrapped the child in the cold wet sheet and took her upstairs to place her in bed. The children had been playing bear. They had scared the baby into backing up and she backed right into the opening along the pipes and slipped to the hot stove below. They were all blaming each other as to who did what and Pauline was sick at heart. She did not know what else she could do for the baby girl. Anne eventually fell asleep and Pauline went down and continued to do her laundry. Pauline was fourteen years old.

It was starting to get windy as Anna and Metro rode along. The snow was also beginning to fall again. She was getting very restless and told Metro to hurry the horses along. She had a gut feeling that something terrible had happened and she could not wait to get home.

Anna and Metro finally arrived in the yard. It was late afternoon. Anna had a premonition. She was also very impatient. She left the wagon immediately for Metro to tend to and ran into the house. She stood in the doorway and asked Pauline what happened. Pauline was shocked that her mother would know that something had indeed happened and explained to Anna about her baby sister. Anna rushed upstairs to the sleeping infant and examined her closely. She was horrified and kept praying to God all the while.

Anna had made some home made salve which she used for just about everything. It was her own concoction. She placed the salve generously on cabbage leaves and covered all Anne's burned skin with these cabbage leaves. She then wrapped her up in clean sheets. She used the cotton sheets as she did not want the wool to possibly cling to the scalded areas of the baby's body. Besides, the cotton tended to have a cooling effect on burned skin. She praised Pauline for her actions in applying the butter to the blistered parts and because the butter had salt in it, this probably prevented the areas from getting infected.

The following Saturday, the wedding guests once more came to Anna's place to finish off the remainder of the food from the wedding. They had all heard about Anna's daughter getting scalded and went upstairs to view the child. They told Anna that the baby should be in hospital as she would not survive. Anna paid them no mind and kept applying her salve on cabbage leaves and slowly healed Anne back to health. Once again, the neighbours were in shock and were utterly amazed by Anna's healing abilities.

Mary Kuzyk and Steve Toporowski Wedding Day

Chapter 18

High Off the Hog

That winter of 1932 was pretty hard on Anna and Metro. Mary was married and had her big wedding. It took a great deal of their savings though and left them with very little money for the cold winter months.

It was their first Christmas in their new house. Anna prepared the usual Christmas meals. The girls made the perogies. Mary and her husband came down for a visit and seemed to be getting along just fine. Mary appeared radiant and was very happy. Anna was pleased with the newlyweds. They had acquired a homestead not too far away and were making plans for the spring planting.

Anne was well on the road to recovery and all that was visible on her tiny body was a scar on her hip.

The following spring Anna decided that they had better do something about the gravel pits. The winter had been long and hard on them and they needed to make some money to live on.

Metro and Anna went into Fork River to see Mr. Ogryzlo about the gravel pits. Mr. Ogryzlo advised them that he would get in touch with the contractor with whom he had been dealing with. He said he would have him get in contact with Anna and Metro about the possibility of signing a contract for the purchase of the sand and gravel.

A few days later a distinguished gentleman appeared at the farm and met with Metro and Anna about purchasing the sand and gravel for cement and the roadways. Upon further discussions a contract was signed whereby Metro and Anna would sell the gravel to the company in question. Also included in the contract was a clause stipulating that Anna would have to prepare one meal a day for the men for as long as it took to fulfil their contract, for an additional sum of money. Anna and Metro agreed to this.

They immediately slaughtered a pig and Anna utilized every portion of the animal. She made pork sausage out of the casings and they were very tasty. She even made some soap out of a portion of the animal and used it for her laundry. Nothing was wasted from the animal. The balance of the pig was reserved for the men working at the gravel pits. Anna smoked most of the pork to preserve it during the summer months.

The day arrived and Anna and the girls cooked a big roast pork, mashed potatoes and gravy and of course, Anna had plenty of home made bread and butter. The girls also made some rhubarb pie for dessert. Sometimes for a change of diet, Anna would kill a few chickens and they would have roast chicken as an alternative. It was a fine arrangement and Anna was quite pleased about the agreement.

The house got terribly hot during the cooking periods. It was summer but they needed the stove to cook the meals and so the stove was constantly going from early morning till late afternoon.

They stayed on the job for about two months and still there was plenty of gravel in the pits. One pit had slowly filled up with water upon being excavated. The men left when they were finished and their contract had been fulfilled. Anna and Metro made plans for the following year to sign another contract. The smaller children would go down to the gravel pits and play in them. Anna warned them about the water and they did not go near the one pit.

Metro was very pleased with the outcome of the contract and Anna especially was happy to make so much money to put away towards the mortgage. She still plastered houses when she could and between what they made on the sale of the gravel and the plastering, she had enough to pay for all the buildings on the property. They had by this time completed the chicken coop and the pig pen. During the winter months, the pigs were moved into the warm barn and a pen was provided for them just for this purpose.

Metro had a well dug in the back of the house and it produced very good water. Anna used the well to keep her butter and other food cool during the summer months. Anna was very pleased with the way things were going and she was in a way, thankful to Mrs. Broschuk for intervening in the old homestead.

There was a pie social in Fork River and Michael told Anna that he would like to go to it. Anna gave him four dollars and this was more than enough for him to buy a box at the social. Michael was a very generous individual. He wanted to eat with a special girl at the pie social. He had some money of his own with him as well. Normally the boxes sold for $1.00 to $1.50 and when the box of food was being bid on that belonged to the girl Michael was interested in, he bid $6.00 on it which was all the money he had with him. He had his box social with the girl and that was all that mattered.

When he got home and told Anna how much he had paid for the box social, she was furious with him. All that money just for sitting with a girl and eating her pie. Anna could not believe Michael and she continued to scold him for it. Michael was twenty years old and was embarrassed to be chastised by Anna at his age.

Anna and Metro went to Fork River one day and Pauline was left in charge of the household again. Andrew was bored and got an idea. He opened wide the root cellar door. He grabbed Stella, who was just four years old, and pretended to throw her into the big dark root cellar. Stella screamed in terror as Andrew continued to threaten to cast her into the darkness. Pauline finally intervened and he let the child go.

Andrew kept telling Pauline to pour the wax over Stella and see if it would reveal anything. Pauline was worried for Stella who was crying hysterically. She got the pan Anna normally used for her wax ritual and Andrew held it over the little girl's head while Pauline poured the hot

Chapter 21

Garden of Weedin'

It was a pretty piece of property, Anna thought to herself. She and the old woman had almost reached an agreement. The property was on the outskirts of Fork River on the main road out of town. It was a corner piece situated on an acre of land. It had an old barn, which Anna was not too happy with, but there was room behind the old barn for a new one to be built if one so desired. There was also a small granary and an outhouse. The nice thing about it was the entire property had a fence around it. The house itself was not much to speak of though. In fact, it was really nothing more than a one room shack. Nevertheless, it would have to do.

In the town of Fork River there were four general stores, a school, two grain elevators, a post office, a hotel and a gas station at the entrance of town. There was also a depot and a train came through the town once a day. A large community hall was situated across the road from the school where weddings and dances were held. Anna was also very happy about one of the two churches. There was an Anglican church and a small Polish Roman Catholic church, to which a priest from Dauphin came to say mass once a month.

The old woman wanted to sell as soon as possible and was anxious to complete the transaction. Anna had saved the money sent to her by the five children from Flin Flon which could be used to buy the property with.

The elderly lady and Anna had met in one of the general stores. They had discussed the sale of the place. Anna had gone to view the property on a whim, but it suddenly occurred to her that it would be nice to be in town. A few more years and Anna would be fifty years old. The farm was not looking too prosperous to her.

The school was close by as well and that would mean the smaller children would not have to miss any school in case of a storm or blizzard in the winter. There was Johnny, Bill, Sonia, Peter, Stella and Anne still at home. Stella was just five years old and was not ready to start school yet. Anne was a year and a half younger.

Anna and Metro fought over the idea of moving into town. They had bartered the cow for some sheep recently and Anna had to go to one of the neighbours to get her daily milk supply for the children. This did not make her very happy, but at the time the sheep were important both to her and Metro.

Metro maintained he would not give up his sheep or the farm. They did not put in the garden that spring, so Anna insisted, there was no reason for them to stay on the farm. It was one of the few times that Metro stood his ground. This was very perturbing to Anna who always had her way. Anna was very ambitious. She had her mind made up.

One day she hitched up the oxen, they had since replaced the horses, and rode into Fork River to meet with the old woman. Together they went to see Mr. Ogryzlo, who was also a lawyer and discussed the deal with him. The price was fixed and it was agreed that Anna could have possession almost immediately. Anna purchased the property for seventy five dollars.

So it was on a warm spring day in 1935, Anna, with the help of Metro and the boys, loaded up the wagon with a couple of beds, the kitchen stove, a sack of potato eyes for seed and other precious seed for planting which Anna needed. They also loaded up the trunk with her feather tick and pillows among other things. They set out to make the journey into town. Metro remained behind with the sheep and refused to go along with them. Anna did not care what the neighbours would be thinking. If it meant a separation, so be it. She was doing it for the children.

With the help of the five children in Flin Flon, Anna speculated, and the money they sent her, she would build a barn on her new property and buy herself a cow. The place was just the right size for a nice big garden and this made Anna very happy. She had to have a garden. The soil was rich with black loam she had noted. She had great plans for her new place.

Anna wasted no time in getting her garden in. It was late spring, she knew, but better late than never. The boys ploughed the land with the oxen and Anna seeded her garden. She also proceeded to build a pyatz, and she gathered the horse manure for it. The pyatz was built along side the house. Again, it was a labour of love to her.

She also had a chicken fence put in alongside the granary and purchased a few chickens, some turkeys and a couple of geese. A makeshift chicken coop was built along one side of the granary. She still needed a cow, but for now she would buy her milk from one of the neighbours.

There was no well but the Mossey River meandered close by and this would be sufficient to meet Anna's needs. In the winter time she would melt the snow like she had always done in the past for her water supply. Anna was extremely happy with the way things were progressing.

It was almost a month now since Anna and the children moved into town. They had settled down nicely and everything was going well. The older children were attending school and were able to move about town making new friends and Anna was quite content. Many a night though, she would worry and wonder how Metro was doing. So one evening, leaving the older children in charge, she packed some bread and chicken into a sack, flung it over her shoulder and set out on the three mile trip to the farm.

Anna was compulsive and did things on the spur of the moment. She did not know why she chose to go to the farm at night, but go she knew she must. Darkness had already set in as Anna plodded along rapidly down the main road out of Fork River. She then proceeded about a half a mile along the dirt road to the double pathway in the bush. This was the part of the trip Anna liked the least. It was a half mile of bush that always made her feel queasy. It was a moonless night. The clouds were dark overhead. It was almost pitch black when suddenly, he appeared out of nowhere, a tall man with an equally tall black hat on his head. He was wearing a black suit which blended in with the darkness outside. They almost collided with each other. He appeared like an apparition. He seemed so out of place in the bush. He belonged on a stage singing an aria Anna thought. They both stopped dead in their tracks, inches from each other. Neither said a word for what seemed like minutes.

Finally Anna looked up at the man and uttered a "good day" to which the man in the tall hat echoed back at her. They stood staring at each other, still neither one of them moved. It was incredible! Anna seemed to be paralysed with fear. Suddenly she got enough courage to move and quickly side-stepped the man and continued on her way. She dared not glance over her shoulder but proceeded briskly along, almost running.

She calmed down some as she went, realizing that probably the man had been just as frightened of her as she was of him when they confronted each other. Anna laughed nervously to herself as she thought about the encounter, and continued on her way to the farm. An idea formed in her mind. She would play a trick on Metro when she got to the farm.

The familiar scene appeared in the darkness, there was the house. She walked by the pyatz and a sadness came over her. She would not be using it again. It had served her well.

There were no lights on in the house and Anna assumed that Metro was in bed. She opened the door ever so carefully and then knocked loudly. After a few seconds, Metro yelled out asking who was there but Anna did not answer him. In the quiet of the night she could hear

Metro sharpening his knife and then coming down the squeaking stairs. Anna made herself known to Metro at this point. The joke had gone far enough. Metro was surprised and overjoyed to see her and Anna stayed the night.

Anna told Metro all about her new home. How she had built the pyatz and the chicken coop. How her garden was coming along. She also told him of her plans to build a new barn behind the old one and the cow she wanted to get. He was very impressed and listened quietly as Anna rambled on. Metro had lost some weight and Anna was very concerned about him.

The next day Anna prepared to return to Fork River. They had not discussed the move by Metro but Anna had high hopes that he would not stay on the farm much longer.

On her return trip, Anna managed to capture a wild duck and some little ducklings. She placed them in her sack and brought them home. She clipped the duck's wings and released them in the chicken coop. The duck did not fly away but stayed with her little ducklings. This was a good omen to Anna.

A week or so later, Metro sold his sheep and came to Fork River giving up the farm. It was an extremely hard decision for him to make but he knew he could not manage without Anna. Anna, however, was content and happy with his move.

They decided to forfeit the farm and the mortgage payments were no longer being made on it. Subsequently, the farm was foreclosed on. It was rumoured that eventually the farm sold but Anna had enough of the struggle with it and was content to take the loss.

Metro and Anna's New Fork River Home

Chapter 22

And Don't Come Back!

That fall, Anna's garden produced well. She and the boys, Johnny, Bill and Peter, managed to dig up all the potatoes and the younger children helped with filling up the sacks. They munched on carrots as they were picked and carried the cabbage into the house to the root cellar. The cucumbers had been picked earlier and were in the granary soaking in brine. Soon Anna surveyed the situation and decided that she was ready for the coming winter.

The house was full of flies. With the opening of the door in getting the vegetables into the house, the flies had a picnic. Anna would get up early in the morning before the children arose and with the fly swatter, she would swat away at the flies while the children slept. Every so often, she would smack one of the children in the process of killing a fly and wake them up. Anna could not stand the terrible insects.

The threshing of wheat in the area was completed by the farmers. The hay was mowed and huge haystacks loomed everywhere. The older boys decided to build a tunnel in one of the haystacks. It had rained, the hay had settled and was easy to scoop out. They dug their way through the entire haystack from one end to the other and then played hide and go seek in it. When Anna found out that even the younger children were involved, she was horrified! It was very dangerous, she scolded, as the hay could have collapsed in on them at anytime and they could have suffocated. Anna forbade the children to go anywhere near the haystack again.

Anna worried about her young daughter. Stella cried continually. She would sob her heart out as she lay on the ground beside the barn. She would do this constantly. Mrs. Briggs, the next door neighbour came over to Anna one day and asked her what was wrong with the child. Anna merely shrugged her shoulders and said she did not know. No one knew why Stella cried so much, not even Stella herself.

That winter Anna became acquainted with some of the ladies in town who had a quilting bee. Anna joined them for something different to do and every week the ladies would gather at the Chornoboy's place and work on a quilt.

One day when Anna was in town visiting, Stella, who was not yet going to school, decided she wanted to go sliding down the hill towards the river. She and Anne did not have rubbers for their feet because they did not go to school yet. Anna could only afford rubbers for those who went to school. The younger children remained bare foot in the summer and stayed indoors in the winter. Times were very hard for Anna and her family. They no longer had the wheat money to rely on for the winter months. She only had the money sent to her by the children in Flin Flon to live on.

Bare feet, Stella grabbed the sled and ran the distance in the snow to the top of the hill and slid down. Then she hurriedly ran back up the hill to the house to get her little feet warm. She would then run out and repeat the procedure over again. Her feet were almost frozen doing this and she finally got into bed under the feather tick to keep warm and fell asleep. Anna did not find out and Stella did not tell her mother what she did as she knew she would get a spanking for it.

During the winter months Anna had time to do some cooking. The potatoes had lasted through the winter and Anna made plenty of potato soup and borscht from the beets. She often had chicken soup on Sundays instead of perogies because she did not have the girls to help her and making the perogies took too long. They also had sauerkraut which Anna made in a ten gallon crock. She would fry the sauerkraut with onions until it turned a golden brown and the children loved it.

Anna made cabbage rolls but only on special occasions. There was no meat in the cabbage rolls, just rice but the children loved them anyway. They were a real treat. Anna always had fresh bread in the house too. It was a pretty good winter as far as food was concerned and the children had plenty to eat.

Anna also spent a great deal of time with the stemming of the feathers and Metro would read to her as he normally did. He was still getting the weekly newspaper from Winnipeg and there were usually some steamy love stories in it and Anna loved a good romantic tale. Metro was happy not to have to worry about going into the bush to chop wood. They had their wood delivered to them for a change. The winter supply of wood was piled up along side the house and all he had to do was step out the door and retrieve it.

There was a new game out called Parcheesi. The children would ask Anna to buy the game for them. It would be a game that would keep them busy during the winter months when there was nothing else to do in the house they insisted. Bill cut out a piece of cardboard and drew the game on it. He then got a piece of wood and carved out a set of dice and numbered each one. They used buttons for men. The children were joyous over the new game and Anna was grateful to Bill for his taking the initiative.

The following spring, 1936, Anna once more got her garden in early. She was short of seed one day and approached a bachelor in the valley for some. His name was Soloway. He lived by himself but he also appreciated a good large garden. He advised Anna that he was interested in drama. This perked Anna's ears right up. She became very friendly with him and spent some time with him that summer talking about her participation in plays. Anna told him all about her acting experiences in the old country. He was teaching drama at the school and worked with the children at Christmas time with their plays and the singing of

Christmas carols. Metro became extremely jealous of Anna's acquaintance with Mr. Soloway, and they argued about it constantly.

There was an old gentleman by the name of Storey, who lived at the other end of town and he was alone also. He was in his eighties and Anna made his acquaintance too. Anna was a very compassionate woman and cared about elderly people. Mr. Storey often needed help getting wood into the house for the winter and numerous other chores which needed to be executed. Anna would send the boys down to the Storey place and they would do what was required of them. Mr. Storey would give the boys a dime now and again.

He appreciated what was done for him. He would come down to Anna's place every Saturday with the Winnipeg Free Press paper and the comics section. The boys loved to keep up with the Tarzan series and looked forward to the next episode. Sometimes the boys would stay overnight with the old man and Anna did not object.

That summer there was a plague of army caterpillars. They were all over everything. There was hardly a spot where one could stand without squishing them. It was a disgusting sight to the children. The caterpillars ate everything in sight. They were on the roads, in the grass and in the woods. Anna was worried about her garden, but miraculously, her garden survived.

One bright sunny afternoon, there was a knock on the door. Anna answered and discovered a woman standing on her doorstep. She had a book and some other material with her. A discussion ensued and the lady advised Anna that she was a Jehovah's Witness. They began arguing about religion and the woman stood her ground and insisted that her version of the bible was the correct one. Anna became exceedingly annoyed with the woman and told her outright to leave her premises. The Jehovah's Witness continued to argue. Frustrated, Anna picked up the broom and swung it in anger at the woman. The frightened lady turned and fled in terror. Anna chased her down the road a ways before she finally returned to the house. She was still fuming and talking to herself as she continued to do her chores. Metro would only smile and the dimple would appear in his left cheek. This was his Anna, his little ball of fire.

Peter, Bill, Sonya in Back, Stella and Anne in Front

Chapter 23

Radio Rock Stars

The garden was the envy of the town. The rows were straight and every plant was uniform. Even strangers would stop and admire it. Anna was very proud and tended to spend a great deal of time with her garden.

Metro's illness prevented him from doing the things he wanted to do, like getting the wheat in. They decided to try their hand at farming again. They rented a piece of land across the road from the house. They planted the wheat with the help of Johnny and Bill with the two oxen. There were no neighbours to help them and come threshing time they found it a real hardship. They had to hire help and this left them with very little money once the wheat was sold. They decided to give up farming entirely.

They bartered the oxen, the children had named them Bill and Charlie, for a cow and a couple of pigs. The children called the cow Whitey because it was entirely white. Anna was pleased to finally have a cow and milk and butter of her own for the children. She would merely hand over a quart jar to one of the children and tell them to shake it until the butter was made.

The children were cramped in the small house. Anna and the girls slept in the one bed in the corner. The boys slept in the other bed and Metro's cot was beside the table and the four chairs. Metro had not shared the bed with Anna since the move to Fork River. The big kitchen stove was across the room in the corner by the window.

Anna persuaded Metro to write to the boys in Flin Flon and ask them to send some money to help with the building of a new barn. Anna hired a carpenter to do the work and soon the barn was on the way to completion.

Michael and Andrew were working in the bush cutting wood across the lake from Flin Flon. During the summer months they would chop the wood and during the winter months, they would haul it by truck over to the mainland. They drove the trucks across the ice. This frightened Anna and she told Metro to write and tell the boys to find another job.

Fred was delivering bread for Mr. Flocks and his bakery by horse and wagon. Pauline and Jessie were now waitresses in a local Chinese restaurant in this mining town.

The children also wrote that Pauline and Jessie were now singing and playing the guitar on radio once a week. The radio station was CFAR Flin Flon, Manitoba. It was too bad that Anna did not have a radio so she could hear them sing. They had a half hour program and were getting quite a few fans writing to them. Anna was overwhelmed with joy at this news. She always knew her family was talented.

Pauline wrote and advised that she had also purchased a sewing machine for herself. It was an electric one and she was learning how to sew. She had made a couple of black jumpers for Jessie and herself and they looked like twins in them.

The new barn was finished and the old barn remained standing. Anna stored the hay in the old barn. The pigs were also kept in the old barn. She kept the cow in the new barn and Metro thought that the structure was just a waste of money for just one cow. Anna argued that she had plans to perhaps get another cow in the near future.

All the children except Anne were now attending school and this gave Anna more time to do other things. She met a lot of the townspeople and in particular, the wife of the hotel owner, Mrs. Burtniak. She did the cleaning in the hotel for the Burtniak's. She cleaned the pub and the rooms. The hotel did not have very many guests. The more permanent guests were the two teachers who taught school.

Anna also plastered a house in the neighbourhood, using the same method as she used for her pyatz. She would plaster in between the logs and smooth it out level so that all the cracks were covered. Later she whitewashed it and the house looked very impressive. A few of the townspeople noticed Anna's work and by word of mouth, it soon got around and she was plastering other homes in the area. This brought in a few dollars, but it was not sufficient to feed and clothe the entire family.

That winter Anna awaited the birth of her first grandchild. She had so many things on her mind but she was also concerned about Mary. On November 23, 1936, Mary gave birth to a son. She named him Peter after his uncle. The child was healthy and Anna thanked God again. Anna and Metro went to visit Mary and her newborn. Anna pressed a silver dollar into the infant's hand. A symbol of wealth to come. Anna was very happy.

It was a few years since the stock market crash of 1929. The economy had not improved. The depression had not affected Anna and her family too much though. They were poor before and they were still poor now.

Anna had applied to the government for assistance through Mr. Ogryzlo, but to no avail. She had previously applied to him for help when they were still on the farm. At that time she received a cheque for three dollars. The cheque had been left on the dining room table by Anna. The wind blew the cheque on the floor and Jessie, who had been sweeping the floor, swept the piece of paper up and burned it. Anna had to re-apply for the money again. For some reason the government refused her any more assistance after that. It was a one time effort on the part of the government.

It was during the summer holidays. Anna found it necessary to send Stella over to Mary's place. Pauline had arrived for a visit from Flin Flon and Anna wished Mary to know this. Little Anne accompanied Stella and together they set out for Mary's farm. They spent the better part of the day at their older sister's place. Mary made sure they got away early enough to reach home before dark.

It was about five o'clock in the afternoon when they reached the outskirts of Fork River just in front of the gas station. Anne was wearing a sandy coloured coat and it blended in with the gravel on the road. It happened so quickly. The car struck Anne and before Stella realized what had happened, there was Anne lying very still on the road. Stella thought Anne was dead. She dashed away from the site, across town and home as fast as her little legs could carry her. Anna was working in her garden. Pauline was scrubbing the floor in the house. Anna knew something was dreadfully wrong when Stella arrived home panting and out of breath. Stella said repeatedly that the car killed Anne. Anna dropped everything, screamed for Pauline and together, the three of them ran through town to the scene of the accident in front of the gas station. In the meantime the owner of the gas station had already arranged for the transportation of Anne to the Dauphin hospital. The deaf-mute who had struck the little one, was standing by crying softly. There were so few cars in the area that it was incredible that one should have struck the child. Anna was bewildered.

Anna left Pauline in charge and went with little Anne to Dauphin. They did not know whether she would live or die. Anna stayed in the hospital with her baby for three days. When she returned, she related that Anne had come out of her coma and had spoken to her. On awakening, Anne had noticed all the nurses in white around her and thought she was in heaven. Anna was overjoyed, and once again knelt down and thanked God.

Meanwhile, the police were investigating the accident scene to see if criminal charges should be laid against the deaf-mute. The Mountie came to the house and questioned Stella extensively. Stella was frightened, being just seven years old, but answered all the questions carefully.

Pauline was still there and reassured Stella. No criminal charges were laid against the deaf-mute.

When Anne was released from the hospital and arrived home, Anna kept a close watch on her. Stella carried her baby sister piggy back everywhere they went and felt somehow responsible for what had happened to her little sister. She always felt as though she had to look after her younger sibling.

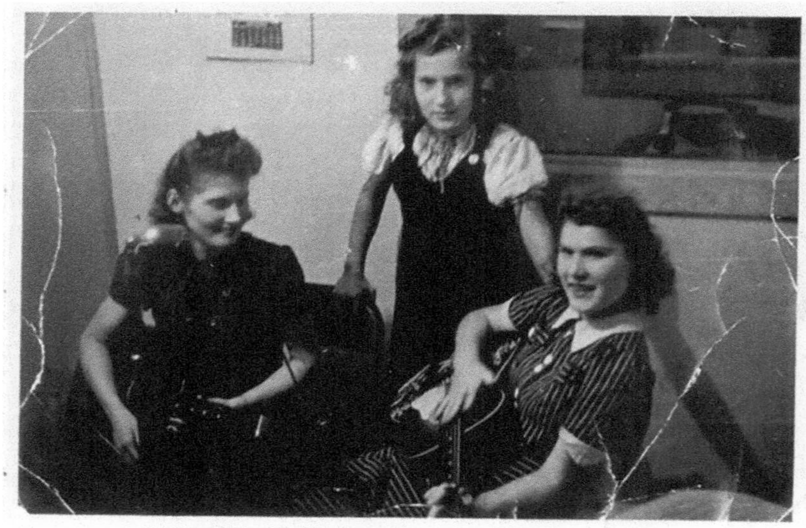

Pauline, Sonia With Stella at CFAR Radio Station

Chapter 24

The Church Lady

It was approximately two years now since Anna had moved to Fork River. Spring of 1937 had arrived early and this enabled her to put her garden in early as well. The garden was the most important function for Anna every spring. It was still the envy of the town. Anna would hill the potatoes and hoe the garden for weeds on a daily basis.

The chokecherry season had approached. The black cherries appeared everywhere. The children's faces were stained with traces of the chokecherries. They stuffed themselves and then they developed terrible stomach aches. Anna would attempt to cure the stomach aches by giving the children a tablespoon of home made moonshine mixed with black pepper. This would settle the stomach Anna insisted and especially, it would stop the diarrhea.

One Sunday she met a lady at the little Polish church and they began speculating on the possibility of having their own Ukrainian church someday in Fork River. Anna invited the lady over and they continued their discussions and talked of nothing else except their dream of a new church. There was this 2.5 acre piece of property a few doors down from Anna's place and wouldn't it be ideal as a site for a new church, Anna pondered out loud.

The conversation went further and one day her new friend and Anna arranged transportation and went to see the Bishop in Dauphin. The Bishop was rather intrigued with the idea of a new church in this small town. He did not wish to commit to anything however. He told Anna and her friend that if they could collect enough money to buy this piece of property, a new church might then be considered. Anna and her friend set out immediately to get pledges or money for the property. They were surprised at the response. Before they knew it, they had enough money for the piece of property in question. Once again, they went to Dauphin to see the Bishop. He was impressed with their enthusiasm and agreed that the church would make arrangements to purchase the property. This in fact, he did and the church purchased the piece of land.

The ladies were ecstatic with the results. They proceeded in earnest now to obtain pledges and money for the new church. The Bishop had set an amount to be collected and then the balance would be funded by the church. Anna and her friend set out to meet the Bishop's requirements. Once again, the response was unbelievable! It was a hardship at times for Anna and her friend because they had to walk a great distance between farms. Sometimes they trudged in the pouring rain but they did not mind. It was easier for them in town but when they had to go to the outlying areas, a neighbour with a car was usually asked to drive them.

Anna would be away on a daily basis. The garden was neglected and she instructed the older children to tend to it. It was looked after but not as well as it should have been and Anna became irritated with Metro and the children. She could not be everywhere at once she admonished. Pretty soon arguments broke out with Metro over her absence. Anna was insistent though and continued with her work of collecting pledges and money for her new church. It was God's work she was doing and it came before all else.

Anna and her friend were excited. It was just four months into the project and already they had collected the amount required by the Bishop for the start of the building of the church. They had met their quota. The Bishop was quite fascinated with the response they were getting for a new church and decided to commit to the building of the structure.

A committee was formed for the future church consisting of ladies in the area and they appointed Anna as their "first sister". Her friend was selected as sister number two. Anna held her head high and was very proud. She threw herself into the project completely and tended to neglect her family even more. Metro was left in charge at home, but he had strict instructions from Anna about disciplining the children. She forbade him to touch any of them. The committee selected a contractor to start the building of the church that fall. There was a great deal of discussion in the town. Anna was the talk of Fork River. Everywhere she went, there were deliberations about the new building. Plans were already being made for the first service next summer. Anna came to the site every day to assess the progression of the structure. She was very pleased with the results.

Anna's garden survived and that fall she worked hard to get her garden in for the winter. The older children helped her with the harvest and soon she had her vegetables in the root cellar.

There was a lot of jealousy over the appointment of Anna as the top sister. One day Anna received a letter from persons unknown about her and Metro. It was a poison pen letter. Anna and Metro would be whispering about this letter all the time. Anna's cousin John Rozmarnowich and his wife were aware of the contents of the letter. They too were very secretive about it. There were rumours about town that Anna had poisoned Metro and that was the reason for his illness. The children were very curious but that was the extent of their knowledge about the contents of the letter. There were more letters received by Anna. She was strong though and continued to be involved in the new church. She said that the devil himself was trying to intervene with the building of the new church. It was the work of the devil, but she had God on her side and He would help her. Anna would pray every night for strength and somehow managed to survive the ordeal of the letters.

It was suggested that she should take the letters to the police and have them investigate the matter. Anna refused to do this. She said that she would look after it herself. She had her suspicions as to who was writing them, but only she and Metro conversed privately about it.

The following summer the building of the church was almost complete and work on the interior was beginning to shape up. Arrangements were being made for the grand opening. During the summer holidays when school was out, a priest came down to Fork River and taught catechism to the children outdoors by the still unfinished church. Anna's children attended the catechism lessons. Anna was very happy. It was a great feeling. She had accomplished so much and was again, very proud.

Later that summer they had their first mass at the new church. Anna's dream became a reality. The people from every corner of Fork River attended. There was a huge procession and everyone paraded all around the church while the Bishop blessed it. He was dressed in fine brightly coloured robes. Anna being the first sister with her friend the second sister, followed closely behind the Bishop. They both sang the responses to the Bishop's chanting in clear and loud voices. The congregation was behind them and they too had their turn in the chanting. It was a beautiful day and the people were very enthusiastic. Anna's heart was near bursting with pride and joy. Stella made her first holy communion there. The church, St. John The Baptist Ukrainian Greek Catholic Church is now a Manitoba Historical site.

Jim Duschl at St. John the Baptist Church Fork River

Chapter 25

Flu Epidemic

Anna made preparations for the children to start school. She bartered chickens, pigs, butter and eggs for whatever they needed for the coming fall. She had very little else to bargain with at the local stores. Anna worked everything on a barter system. One day she sent Stella to the store with a dozen eggs to exchange for a box of precious wooden matches. They used matches for the pyatz, the stove and the coal oil lamps. The children did their home work by the light of the coal oil lamps.

The school was a two room building. One room was taught by a Miss Barnes, teaching grades one through eight. The other room was occupied by a Mr. Slobodzian, who taught grades nine through twelve and was the principal. There was a cloak room in each of the two rooms. The basement was a huge area taking in both the rooms above. This area was used by the children in the winter time as a play area at recess. There were also two out houses, one for boys and one for girls.

All of Anna's children were in the classroom taught by Miss Barnes. One day Stella was passing a note to Johnny and the teacher caught her. She told both Stella and Johnny to stay after school at which time she advised them that Mr. Slobodzian would be giving them both the strap. Stella was terrified. She had never been strapped before. She was especially petrified of the male teacher. Johnny tried to console Stella and when they appeared before Mr. Slobodzian he asked them why they were there. Stella began to cry and told him about the note passing incident. She told him that it was her fault because she wrote the note. He reprimanded both of them and then advised Stella that she must give the strap to Johnny and he to Stella. This was very unusual. Johnny held out his hands and Stella lightly strapped his hands. Then Stella held out her hands while Johnny strapped her. After this encounter, Stella adored the male teacher and thought he was a very nice man. When they got home and told Anna about it however, she was ready to give them a strapping too. She was very strict and believed in discipline. If her children were punished at school for something they did, then they would also get it at home later.

That winter a flu epidemic broke out. The school was very concerned about it and a vaccination program was instituted. Every child was to be vaccinated at a cost of one dollar per child. Anna had six children in school and could not afford to pay such an exorbitant amount. Mrs. Lacey, who was even poorer than Anna's family, had many boys also. She was on government relief and could not afford to pay this amount either. Her husband had left her and they lived in a small shack across the river from Anna's place. When the doctor came to the school to administer the shots, the Lacey boys and Anna's children were excluded. So it was, if you were rich you survived, if you were poor, you died.

It was a bad winter for Anna and the children. The children caught the flu and Stella had the whooping cough so bad that she could hardly catch her breath in between coughing spasms. She thought that she was going to die. The other children also contacted a severe case of chicken pox, which might not have been so serious had they received their vaccination. Anna got out her garlic again and mashed it into juice. She applied it to their bodies on the chest, back and palms of their hands. The smell of garlic in the tiny house reeked. It worked though and the children improved.

It was a bitterly cold winter. The children missed a great deal of school that year being home sick. The frost would form on the inside of the two windows in the house. The children would scratch pictures and write on the frosted windows. They would also blow on the window and rub the frost off so that they could see outside. Somehow the winter passed and all the children survived in spite of the lack of vaccination.

That summer Andrew wrote home and advised the family that he would be coming for a visit. He also appraised them that a bicycle he ordered from the catalogue would be arriving a week before him at the train depot. He instructed the boys to please pick it up for him. Sure enough, the bicycle arrived and Bill and Johnny picked it up and put it together. All the children had a chance to ride the bicycle for a week before Andrew appeared on the scene. He was furious. It was a brand new bicycle and he had wanted to be able to try it out himself first. Anna chided him for it and pretty soon Andrew stopped complaining. He rode all over town on the bicycle and when he left, he took it with him to Flin Flon. The children were saddened by this, as they had hoped he would leave the bicycle behind.

Johnny was almost seventeen years old and decided school was not for him. He wanted to go to Flin Flon and work like the others. One day he wrote to the older boys and requested they send him his fare to Flin Flon. Shortly, Johnny too was gone. He got himself a job at one of the movie theatres ushering and collecting tickets.

Bill was fifteen years old and was making money doing odd jobs about town. He had a dime piggy bank into which he deposited all his money. Bill was a good, deeply caring young lad and he exuded with kindness. In some ways, he took after his father. He was quiet, gentle and never complained about anything. One day Anna wanted to buy a pig. She knew of Bill's savings. She removed the three dollars from his bank and bought the pig with it. Bill was very upset but kept his feelings to himself.

One Sunday afternoon, Bill and his friend went to Mary's place for a visit. There was no one at home and so the boys helped themselves to something to eat and decided to wait a while. They noticed a bottle of whisky sitting on the kitchen counter. Bill's friend thought that they should sample a bit of the whisky. They kept sampling it until half the bottle was gone. Bill became deathly ill and brought up all over the floor. His friend passed out and later was sick to his stomach as well. The boys had terrible headaches after that. Bill never touched liquor after that day. The smell of it made him nauseous. He had told Anna about it. Later on in years she was very proud of him for not drinking. Andrew never drank either and Anna often praised both boys for it.

Later that summer Bill and some of the Lacey boys got together. They were loading and unloading a twenty-two. Somehow, Bill got shot in the foot and with a great deal of pain, he managed to walk home with the bullet still in his foot. When he hobbled in and told Anna what had happened, she was horrified! At first she reprimanded him for playing with the gun. Then when she realized the severity of the situation, she immediately arranged for someone to drive Bill to the Dauphin hospital to have the bullet removed. There was an investigation as to the shooting but no charges were laid. It was ruled an accidental shooting and the matter was dropped. Bill was operated on, the bullet was removed successfully and he recuperated at home for a couple of weeks. Anna thanked God that he was shot in the foot only and not somewhere else.

There were a lot of wild animals in the area. In particular, a lot of mink at the river and Anna bought a few traps for Bill as compensation for the money she took from him. He would go out in the blowing snow and set trap lines along the river. He made a few dollars selling the pelts and soon forgot about the three dollars Anna used to buy the pig with.

Bill came home one day from checking his lines and told Anna that someone had stolen his trap and his mink. There was blood in the snow but no trap or animal. There were also human footprints in the snow leading away from the area of where the trap should have been. Anna said she knew who had stolen the mink and trap. It had to be the Inkster lad. He was the only other one in town who was also into trapping. Anna, in spite of the objections of Bill, was determined to do what was right. She went to the Inkster home and confronted the lad with a threat of going to the police if he did not give up the trap and the mink. Frightened, the lad turned over both. He had already skinned the mink but gave Anna the pelt. Anna was content with this and felt justified in her actions. Bill too was happy and resumed his trapping.

Bill, Anna, Metro in back, Peter, Sonia, Anne and Stella in front.

Chapter 26

Superman Sighted

Bill and Peter became good friends with the Lacey boys. They did everything together. Birds of a feather Anna thought. The families were both very poor and had a great deal in common. During the summer holidays, the boys met and agreed to build a swing over the shed at the Lacey place. The Lacey's lived on the river. The river was not very wide at the point where the shed was situated. The group decided that it would be fun to swing across the river on a rope tied to the top of a tree beside the shed. They climbed up the tree and secured the rope to it. They would then climb up the ladder to the top of the shed, grab hold of the rope, jump off the shed and swing across the river like Tarzan on his vine. The river was not deep and, in fact, had a very rocky bottom. All the kids in town would come over and try their hand at swinging across to the other side of the river.

One day a friend of Sonia's thought that she would like to try it. She did not want to hurt her hands on the rough rope however, so she placed her coat around the rope for protection. This was a mistake. She did not have a firm grip on the rope. The coat slowly slipped down the rope when she jumped off the shed and she landed on the rocks below. She cut her knee pretty badly and had to be rushed to the hospital in Dauphin for stitches. All the parents began to complain. They tried to stop their children from going over to the Lacey place. The boys were happy about this because it was not as crowded any more.

There was a great deal of excitement in town. Every child in Fork River was collecting comic books. They were mostly "Superman" comics. The children would trade when they were finished reading them and pretty soon the whole town was trading. Mr. Storey got involved too and would bring comic books to the boys now and again. There was fighting in Anna's family over these comics as to who had the right to be the first to read them. Anna would have to play referee.

Later that summer, Pauline and Jessie came down for their holidays. They brought their guitars with them. Soon the neighbours were coming over to listen to them sing their duets. The whole town, of course, had heard about the girls singing on radio and treated them like celebrities.

It was cranberry season and Anna wanted to make cranberry jam. The girls decided to go out and pick the berries. Pauline, Jessie, Sonia and Stella all went out along the river where most of the cranberry bushes grew. Everything was going well until Jessie came running to the other three and yelled to them that there was a bear in the bush. Apparently, as she was picking the berries, she happened to glance to the other side of the bush and noticed a bear picking and eating the cranberries too. It was downwind and the bear had not seen or smelled Jessie. The girls all decided to quickly give up picking the cranberries and rushed home to safety. They had picked sufficient berries for Anna who made the jam for storage in the granary.

Mrs. Briggs, the elderly lady who lived next door to Anna, had two sons. One had a club foot and his name was Lloyd. The other was called George. They were very decent to Anna and the children. It was George who advised Anna that he wanted a chance to call on Pauline one night. Anna consented and so the girls cleaned up the place in readiness for the evening. He came calling and sat on the bed beside Pauline. She and Jessie sang songs and played the guitar for him. One song in particular he enjoyed was "You are my Sunshine.". He was very infatuated with Pauline. They chatted for a while before he left. He wanted to correspond with Pauline but she was not very interested.

The girls departed for Flin Flon shortly after that. Pauline left her guitar for Peter, who went crazy over it. He actually learned how to play it watching Pauline. He was enthralled with the guitar and carried it with him everywhere he went. He would not let Stella touch the instrument. They would constantly fight over the guitar. She wanted to learn how to play the guitar too, but Peter would not permit it. He tended to be a bit selfish about it and Anna could do nothing to change his mind.

Metro's health was deteriorating since his move to Fork River. He was glad not to have the farm to deal with. His legs were giving him trouble. He was starting to shuffle when he walked. He helped Anna all he could with the chores outside, but mostly, he would sit and read or play cards with the children. Anna was still stemming the feathers and enjoying the stories he would read to her.

Some evenings Metro would also tell bedtime stories to the younger girls. One story in particular he told, was the one of Ali Baba and the Forty Thieves. The girls would curl up on the bed and look up at Metro in fascination while he related the tale. It was such a long story though that it took Metro a week to finish. The girls waited in anticipation for the next evening to hear more about Ali Baba. Metro could spin a good yarn, and the girls loved their father very much for the time he took to tell them these fascinating stories.

The girls wanted to learn how to knit. One day Metro cut some heavy wire into knitting needle lengths, sharpened the ends, and straightened out the wire. Anna had some wool handy and Metro taught the girls how to cast on the stitches and then how to knit. Sonia began on a pair of socks and Metro helped her with them. Anna herself did not know how to knit and she was impressed with her husband.

One day they discovered that the three girls had lice. Sonia and Stella had contacted them at school and soon the scratching of the heads began. Anna would collect water from the river and heat it for their bath. She would then make the girls get into the wooden tub and give them a good scrubbing. Anna would wash their hair, then using a fine tooth comb, she would comb their hair over a newspaper, attempting to get the lice out. But to no avail, the girls still continued to have lice.

The children owned a cat and they named him Muchko. They would fight over who would have the animal to sleep with at night. Anna would caution them that taking the cat to bed was dangerous. Cats had the power to suck the breath away from a child when the child was asleep. Anna was very superstitious but this ploy did not succeed in frightening the girls. They still slept with the cat.

Anna was not an affectionate person. There was never any affection shown between Metro and Anna. At least not in front of the children. She loved her children, but she just did not have the time to spend with them. It was always understood in her household that the older children looked after the younger ones.

Anna would not always be there when the children came home for lunch. She was often away working on a house she was plastering or cleaning at the Burtniak's hotel. Although Anna was busy, she managed to have food in the house for her children. She would barter some chickens for a large ten pound bag of puffed wheat, which was a cereal, for their breakfast and it would last for a long time.

The children would still go out and pick the cranberries for cranberry jam which Anna would make and store in the granary. There was always fresh bread in the house to go with the cranberry jam. The children would run down to the river to get some water and make cold tea to go with the cranberry jam sandwich. In the summer the stove was not burning so there was no way of heating the water for tea. One day Sonia found a worm at the bottom of her tea cup. This made everyone nauseous. They were very careful about their tea after that and looked for worms in the river water.

The winter of 1939, the snow came early and it was heavy. Anna had purchased a pair of felt boots for herself and Metro. The felt reached up well above her knees and was in fact thigh high. The feet were made of rubber. With help from the family in Flin Flon, all the children also had rubbers and snowsuits for the winter.

Anna would make the younger children wear long johns. Then she would wrap their feet with rags, put on their snowsuit and then their rubbers over the rags. They had no socks and the rags were used to keep their feet warm. The children were embarrassed and told Anna so, but she insisted they keep the rags on. She threatened them with a beating if they did not do as they were told.

The boys decided that since they had so much success with the swing that summer, they should try their hand at building a slide at the Lacey place too. They cleared the snow on the hill going down to the river. Then they hauled water and poured it on the hill until it became a sheet of ice. They spent hours shovelling a path along the frozen rivulet wide enough to accommodate a sled. The snow was at least three feet deep on the river. The boys then cleared the snow around as far as the curve in the river. It was almost a quarter of a mile in length. A short path was also made in several places away from the main pathway into little cubicles. They would then slide down the hill with a sled, along the ice pathway on the river and into one of these cubicles and play cops and robbers. If you ended up in the same cubicle as the previous individual, that meant the cops captured the robber.

The children spent most of the winter at the Lacey place. The boys worked hard at keeping the snow clear of the area on the river. Again, every child in Fork River was enjoying the slide. The winter months were, for a change, good for Anna. Her children were occupied and out from underfoot.

That Christmas Bill had saved a few dollars from the sale of the mink pelts. He confided with the other children that he bought Anna a sweater for Christmas. He bought Metro a tin of tobacco. He also chopped down a small tree and they decorated it with coloured crepe paper. Everyone was excited and anticipated the day of the opening of the presents.

Anna made her usual wheat soup, perogies with prunes instead of potatoes, cabbage rolls and of course, round home made bread with raisins.

Not all but most of the people in Fork River celebrated Christmas on the 7th day of January. It was the Ukrainian Christmas they celebrated because most of the community was Ukrainian. The school however, celebrated Christmas day on December 25th. So really the Ukrainian children had the benefit of two Christmas holidays.

The package arrived from Swift Current. It was from aunt Dora. She never missed the children at Christmas time. There were mittens, scarves and toques for them. As was usual, Stella did not receive a present. Dora always forgot about her and in fact, was not aware of the birth of the child. Her sister had so many children, she had lost track. Stella cried and Anna told her to hush up.

Christmas day arrived and the excitement mounted. The children were expecting happiness and joy. Everyone sang Christmas carols and Anna was jubilant. However, when she received her present she was very surprised and scolded Bill for spending his money on a sweater she did not need. There were other places the money could have gone to. She was more upset when Metro opened his present and she discovered he had a tin of tobacco. She took the tobacco tin away and neither Metro nor the children knew what she did with it. Everyone was very disappointed with the outcome. This put a damper on the rest of the day.

New Years day was celebrated on January 14th. The smaller children were permitted to go out on this day with some wheat. They would knock on the door of one of their neighbours, sprinkle a bit of wheat on the floor and recite a poem about sowing the wheat for a better crop next year. For this they would receive a large penny from each household. It was a tradition from the old country. This was more money than any of the younger children had ever seen. Anna let them keep this money or spend it if they wished. They would immediately run to the store and buy a black sucker. They were so yummy.

The following spring, Bill became restless. He was almost sixteen years old and wanted to go to Flin Flon too. Anna was upset as Bill was such a good lad and did everything she asked of him. She knew she would be missing him terribly if he left. Needless to say, the others sent Bill his fare and so he was gone too.

Sonia also wanted to go. She was mature for her age and she heard so much about Flin Flon from Pauline and Jessie, she wanted to quit school and get a job in the big town too. So Anna let her go as well. This left just three at home now, Peter, Stella and Anne.

Burtniak Hotel Fork River

Chapter 27

Missing Anne

The following summer, 1940, Pauline came down for a visit again. She was always concerned about the smaller children. She would bring new dresses for the girls. She would teach Peter new songs with his guitar. Peter was in his glory learning the new tunes. She also taught him how to tune the guitar and he became very good at it. Pauline told her mother that Sonia was part of their singing group. They were now a trio on the radio every week. Anna was delighted. Bill had obtained a job at the movie theatre with Johnny and everyone was doing well.

Michael, who was twenty-six years old, had a girlfriend. He had met this sixteen year old and they were discussing marriage. His girlfriend's name was Jean. Anna's first reaction was that she hoped they would get married in a Catholic church.

Andrew was still single and had no girlfriend. He had changed jobs and was now working for the railway company. He spent most of his time in a shack across the lake from Flin Flon where he worked. The shack was situated along the tracks and it was convenient for him to hop the train each morning to go to work. When he wanted to come to the mainland, he would peddle his bicycle along the railway tracks to a place by the lake. He would ask the man who lived on the lake, to ferry him across in his boat. He was making good money though and Anna was pleased.

Pauline brought along a small portable hand cranking gramophone with her together with some records. She would play the records and the refrains could be heard throughout the house and outside in the garden. Anna was happy to have her daughter home with her. Pauline would play her favourite songs like "Engine Number Nine" and "With his sweetheart so dear stood a brave engineer". Another song she played a lot was "South of the Border Down Mexico Way". The younger girls soon learned the lyrics and were singing the songs too.

Anna had an old steel curling iron lying about the house. Pauline would curl Anne's and Stella's hair with it. She would heat the curling iron in the stove until it got sufficiently hot enough to curl the girls' hair. Then she would reheat the curling iron and repeat the process. The girls looked so pretty. When Pauline went back to Flin Flon, the girls would attempt to curl their own hair. They ended up burning a lot of their hair off as the iron was too hot. Eventually, they learned how to work it and tested the iron on a piece of paper first before applying it to their hair.

Stella being ten years old, was starting to take note of her hygiene. One day, she got a pan of warm water, poured some vinegar into it and washed her hair with it. She then took the fine tooth comb and combed her hair unto a newspaper to get rid of the lice. She repeated this procedure a couple of times a week. One day she was pleased to find that all the nits were gone from her hair. What joy, no more lice! No one told her what to do. She had done this on her own and got rid of the lice.

It was nearing the end of June and school was just about over for the summer holidays. Andrew came to visit. He told Anna when he was leaving that she needed a little rest too. Why not let little Anne come with him to Flin Flon for the summer. Anna could have more time to do other things. Anne would be well cared for and they would get her some new clothes. They would also be sure to send her back before school started. Anne was suddenly gone too! Andrew had talked Anna into taking Anne to Flin Flon with him. He convinced Anna that her baby daughter would be well taken care of and reluctantly Anna let her go with Andrew.

Later when they arrived in Flin Flon, Pauline was amazed to see her baby sister with Andrew. Who would look after her during the day, she asked? She had to work all day and so did the others. She was incredulous. Andrew had not thought about this. Pauline eventually got a baby sitter for Anne and paid for it out of her own pocket.

Stella missed her baby sister but not as much as Anna did. She was very unhappy about her decision. She would mope about the house and garden and constantly urged Metro to write to the family and inquire about Anne. She regretted her decision to let Anne go with Andrew to Flin Flon.

One day Whitey the cow died. No one knew how old the cow was, but there she was dead as a doornail. They could not sell the meat because they did not know what the cow died from. For the same reason, they could not eat the meat themselves. So they had to hire someone to remove the carcass. There was just Peter and Stella at home now and Anna thought, she would have to buy the milk again from a neighbour to meet her needs.

Then suddenly, the dog died too. One Sunday a group of children had been playing baseball out in the field across the road from the house. The dog chased the ball unto the road. A car came by and hit it. The dog died instantly. It was so strange as traffic in automobiles was scarce. If a car went by Anna's place once a week it was a rare occurrence. Yet, here it was, the dog ran unto the road and that split second he was hit by a car. His name was "Puppy" and the children buried it. They wanted to place a cross on it but Anna forbade them to do this. Only people had crosses on their graves she emphasized. Anna being very superstitious, was convinced that her decision to let Anne go with Andrew to Flin Flon was a terrible mistake and these incidents were a bad omen.

Peter and the Lacey boys built a cave one day across the river. They dug a big hole in the ground and removed the dirt. It was a large area inside, with seats of dirt all around the excavation. The area was large enough to accommodate six to seven children. They would often play house inside. When it was not used they would cover the opening with a piece of board to keep animals out. No one thought of the possibility of the dirt caving in and smothering the children inside. Especially when it rained and the ground got soggy. Again, no one told Anna about this as they were used to hearing her objections and kept quiet about it.

Metro made a fishing rod out of some wire attached to a long stick. The wire was looped and made to slip tight when jerked hard enough. The children would go fishing for suckers in the river. They would simply place the loop close to the head of the fish and when it moved forward, they would yank on the stick and the fish would become snared. One day they caught quite a few of the suckers and Anna cleaned and smoked them.

Metro loved fish and was enjoying a meal of the sucker one day when he began to go red in the face. He was gasping for breath. A bone stuck in his throat and he almost choked. Anna was frantic and kept pounding him on his back until he threw up the bone. She was not happy whenever he ate fish after that as she was always expecting him to choke on a bone.

Fork River Train Depot

Chapter 28

Wayward Child

Stella was very lonely without Anne. She had made friends with one of the girls from the general store. Her name was Rosie Momotuik. They did everything together. Rosie and Stella would go to the post office and listen to the older teenagers talk. The teens used to gather at the post office during the lunch hour. The mail generally came in about 12:30 p.m. It was considered the local hangout. The teens would pick up their mail and discuss the events of the day and Stella and Rosie would eavesdrop. Every so often, the teens would chase Stella and Rosie out of the post office.

There was one teen in particular that Stella was afraid of. His name was Steve Derrick. He was almost eighteen years old and was always calling Stella names. He was the big bully in the school and was always threatening to beat her up. The more he bullied Stella the more afraid of him she became and he would get a big kick out of the whole matter. Anna tried to talk to him several times, but he only laughed at her.

Stella also became friendly with a girl named Margaret King. She was the daughter of the family who ran the post office. One day she told Stella that she had to go to church and invited Stella to go along with her. Out of curiosity, Stella went to the little Anglican Church. They had a very interesting service and Stella liked it very much. Not thinking anything more about it, Stella later went home and told her mother about her visit to the Anglican Church. Anna went into a rage. She grabbed the closest thing to her which was the fly swatter and frightened Stella out of her wits. Stella ran out the door with her mother in hot pursuit. Stella had no idea what she did wrong. All she knew was that she had never seen her mother so angry before. She hid in the bushes down by the river and stayed there until it got dark. She was very frightened to stay there any longer and knew she had to go home sometime. So she prepared herself for the worse and headed for the house. Her mother was occupied with other things and Stella made herself as scarce as possible. She hoped that Anna would forget how angry she was. Stella crawled into bed without any supper. Anna in fact had not forgotten. She told Stella never to go to that church again. She was a Catholic and must not attend any other church but her own. Stella was very confused, but she promised her mother that she would never go to the Anglican Church again.

Anna was beginning to have problems in controlling Peter. He was thirteen years old. He did what he wanted and would not listen to her. He was the black sheep in the family Anna thought. He had been missing school lately and sometimes when she tried to punish him, he would actually hit her back! He was belligerent and uncontrollable. Stella was always running to her mother crying about something Peter did to her. Sometimes Peter would leave his guitar at home as he could not take it with him everywhere he went. So when he would catch Stella playing with it, he would beat her for touching it.

Mr. Storey would also complain bitterly to Anna about Peter. He said that Peter was mean to him and would taunt and tease the old man. Again, Anna would try to talk to Peter about it, then she would attempt to lick him, but to no avail. He would not listen. Metro, of course, could do nothing as Anna would not allow him to interfere. Mr. Storey finally told Anna that he did not want Peter's help any more. He would lock his door and refuse to let Peter in. In fact, the old man was afraid of Peter.

One day, in frustration, Anna called on Mr. Lundy. He was an Englishman who drove the children from the outlying areas to and from school. In the winter time especially, he would pick up the children quite early in the morning in a horse drawn semi-covered wagon with a small stove in it to keep the children warm. He was known to have complete control over all the boys and they respected Mr. Lundy. It was to him that Anna went this day and asked if he would come over and give Peter a licking. Peter was at home and refused to do her bidding, she said. She found this very hard to take. All her other children were obedient, why was Peter so different? For a moment she felt like she was no longer at the helm, she was not in charge. This frightened her and suddenly she was feeling a little old.

Mr. Lundy agreed to come to Anna's place to see Peter. When he arrived, Peter crawled underneath the bed and hung on to the springs for support. When Mr. Lundy attempted to get to him, he would move from one end of the bed springs to the other and could not be reached. Finally, Mr. Lundy told Anna that he would have to give it up. But he warned Peter that if he caught him in town he would give him a sound threshing. Peter was scared. Mr. Lundy had Anna's permission to do just that, but this did not change him or his behaviour.

One day Anna chased Peter out the door with a strap. His guitar in hand, Peter went over to the Lacey's place to stay. Mrs. Lacey had very little to eat in the house as it was, she did not need an extra mouth to feed. Their main diet consisted of potato pancakes. However, she did not object to Peter staying there. It was thought that she too was afraid of Peter.

One Sunday afternoon, Anna and Metro were away visiting some friends and had left Stella alone. She was looking out the window when she saw Peter standing on the road. He waved his fist at her not knowing that Anna and Metro were away, and threatened her menacingly. Stella was extremely frightened. There was no lock on the door so she just waited him out. Eventually, Peter left and did not enter the house. Stella was greatly relieved.

Anna had Metro write to the boys in Flin Flon about her wayward son. She appeared at the Lacey's place one day and asked Mrs. Lacey to let Peter come out and talk to her. She had received a ticket from the older boys and they wanted Peter to come to Flin Flon for the balance of the summer and begin school in September in Flin Flon, she told him. Anna thought that this was an excellent idea. Perhaps the boys could straighten Peter out. She certainly could not. Right there and then she took Peter to the train depot. She had his clothing packed and shipped him and his guitar out to Flin Flon. This left Stella alone with her mother and father.

Mike Lundy and His School Wagon Team

Chapter 29

A Real Murder Mystery

Anna received a letter from Mike. He and his girlfriend were very seriously contemplating marriage. She wanted the best for her oldest child she was very eager to meet her first born son's girlfriend.

Anna's cousin John Rozmarnowich, his wife and daughter were homesteading on a farm outside of Fork River. Once a month, usually on the Sunday that mass was said in the new church, they would ride into town to see Anna and Metro and go to church together to hear mass. Anna would prepare a meal for them later and they would all have a good visit and return home in the evening.

One Saturday around noon, Anna was visited by a good friend who was from the same Village as Anna. Her husband was also homesteading on a farm nearby. It was her custom to drop in on Anna for a visit every time she came into town. Her name was Mrs. Lena Dulepka.

They had tea and some bread and Mrs. Dulepka complained that for some reason she was just so exhausted and very sleepy. She had walked into town, did the usual shopping and then had visited Anna. She was an attractive woman, 45 years old, and was short like Anna. Her hair was jet black and very long. She wore it combed back in a bun at the back of her neck. About two o'clock, tired as she was, she finally decided it was time to start back home. They said their goodbyes and Mrs. Dulepka left.

The next day the whole town was buzzing. It was incredible! The entire town was in shock. Mrs. Dulepka's husband had reported her missing! He had waited for her return and when she did not appear at dusk, he set out to look for her by following the route that she would normally take. He did not succeed in finding her. A search party was organized by the police the next day and many people set out to look for her. That July was extremely hot which made it very difficult for the search parties. A tracking dog was brought in on the fourth day, but they could not find her body.

The Mounties questioned Anna when they learned of Mrs. Dulepka's visit there. Anna told them everything she knew about the visit. Mike Budzey, 22 at the time, informed the police that he had seen Mrs. Dulepka near her home the afternoon she went missing and noticed John Rozmarnowich following her. Subsequently, the police held Anna's cousin John Rozmarnowich for questioning.

On Thursday, the fifth day, John Rozmarnowich finally broke down and confessed that he had followed, raped and killed Lena Dulepka. He then led police to a field where her body lay. Mrs. Dulepka often complained to Anna about her fear of walking through a particular field, a short cut to get to her home. Mrs. Dulepka had been raped and beaten about the head and her long hair was dishevelled. Her scalp was partially removed from her head and her small frail body looked pathetic. Apparently, after he had killed Mrs. Dulepka, he wandered around for a long while before he went home late that night. He did not want his wife and daughter to find out what a terrible thing he had done. He picked up an axe and stood over the sleeping forms of his wife and daughter. He had contemplated on killing them both. According to his confession, he knew Mrs. Dulepka was in town that Saturday. He also knew what route she usually took home. He had sat in waiting for her. He said she owed him something and he had finally collected it. He had been in love with Mrs. Dulepka in the old country, but she had spurned him and married another. For this he had raped and killed her.

Anna was in a state of shock when she heard this. John Rozmarnowich was her cousin and a very religious man. She could not believe he would be capable of murder. He was subsequently tried, found guilty and was sentenced to life in prison where he eventually died. Mrs. Lena Dulepka became one of the first persons to be buried in the cemetery of St. John the Baptist Church in Fork River, the very church that Anna was so instrumental in establishing.

Mike and Jean Kuzyk

CHAPTER 30

The Circus Comes To Town

Anna and Metro had more time to do different things. They went visiting a great deal that summer and the place they visited a lot were the Chornoboy's. They were an elderly couple who had a granddaughter that they were raising by the name of Olive. Olive was older than Stella but they became friends nonetheless. Anna would take Stella with them sometimes on their visits, but mostly she would be left at home alone.

Stella was ten years old and would be terrified of the dark. The coal oil lamp would be left on for her. There were no curtains on the windows and no lock on the door. She would get under the covers and her eyes were riveted on the window half expecting someone's face to appear in it. There were many such nights that she would wait for her parents to come home and she would not fall asleep until they returned.

One Sunday afternoon Metro and Anna went visiting after church. Stella stayed at home as usual. She was not afraid because it was daylight. She happened to look out the window and spotted Ukrainec staggering down the road headed towards the house. He would still come to visit Metro and Anna on occasion. Not having any time to run outside, Stella quickly hid under the table which was situated beside the door. She held her breath not daring to make a sound. Ukrainec burst into the house with a bang, staggered towards the bed and flopped on top of it. He lay on his back and immediately began to snore loudly. He was terribly drunk and Stella knew it. Stella was so close to the door, she could have reached out and touched him when he entered. She quietly opened the door and ran towards the barn. She crawled up into the hay loft and hid. She would often play in the hay loft with her paper dolls which she cut out from the Eaton's catalogue. She stayed in the barn, peering through the cracks and waited for the return of Anna and Metro. Just before dusk, they appeared and Stella clambered down the ladder and ran towards them crying. She told them about Ukrainec being in the house and how frightened she had been of him. Anna scolded her and told her nothing would have happened, and that she was making a big to do about nothing.

Anna wanted to go to church one Sunday. Stella told her that she was not feeling very well. Her mother was very suspicious but let her stay at home. Stella just did not feel like going to church that morning. After they had left, Stella made some perogies for their meal. Although she was young, she had often watched her mother make perogies and knew how to make them. When they arrived home, Anna became very upset with Stella. She figured that Stella was not too sick to make perogies but she was too sick to go to church. They ate the perogies just the same and Metro especially was pleased as he almost swallowed them whole, he liked them so much. Anna though, was still critical of Stella for staying home. She had no patience with her daughter and Stella avoided her mother for the rest of the day.

One day a small circus arrived in Fork River. It was just passing through and was only a one night affair. The troupe was staying at the hotel in town. Everyone was excited because there was a real live bear in a cage as part of the act. The evening of the show, Anna took Stella to the circus at the community hall. All the town was there, as it was free.

The trainer of the bear performed some magic first, then he brought out the bear and it danced and did some more tricks. Stella thought it was awesome. Anna was cautious. She had seen bears perform on stage in the old country and was not as enthusiastic as Stella was about the performance.

Later as they were walking home, Anna warned Stella to keep away from all the people operating the circus. They were gypsies and gypsies sometimes stole little children. They wandered around from place to place and never had a home to call their own. No one ever found any of the children they had stolen.

Anna decided that she had enough. She insisted one day that Metro write a letter to the children in Flin Flon. She wanted her little girl back home. She missed Anne very much and decided that her little one belonged with her. She would not take no for an answer. They had to send Anne back to her the following week, Metro wrote. The whole family was trying to keep her little girl from her. She was adamant.

She received a telegram from the children stating the day of Anne's arrival. The train usually came into the station around 12:15 p.m. every day. On the day of her arrival, Stella hurriedly left the house, anxious to see her sister. Anna was already waiting for the arrival of the train. Together they watched it pull into the station.

Suddenly, there she was. As pretty as any little girl in the catalogue, Stella thought as Anne stepped off the train. She had on a short flared sky-blue coat with a matching bonnet. Her hair was curled and she wore white knee socks with a pair of black patent shoes. Stella had never seen anything so pretty in her life except in the Eaton's catalogue. Anna hugged and kissed her little girl until she thought she would smother her.

Stella could not take her eyes off Anne. She followed her everywhere she went. Anna however, kept her baby girl at home with her that day and vowed never to let her go anywhere without Anna again. It was not September yet, school had not started and Anna had a week or so with her baby daughter and she savoured it.

Later that fall, the school had a field day. There was high jumping, races and exercises performed by all the other schools in the surrounding districts. It was a big day in Fork River. Stella and Anne participated in most of the events. They got 15 cents for first place, 10 cents for second and 5 cents for third place. It was Stella's first time for ice cream. She came in second in one of the races in her class and received a dime. The ice cream was a nickel, so she got some change back. What a feeling that was. Later she had another ice cream. Anne too won some money. The ice cream was not so new to her as she had plenty of ice cream in Flin Flon.

War had been declared in 1939. Anna was apprehensive about her sons going to war. The boys wrote that none of them had been called or drafted yet. Anna had Metro write often inquiring about their physical examinations.

Steve Derrick had turned eighteen and he was drafted into the army. Just like that he was gone. Stella was so relieved as she had lived in fear for her life. Later everyone in town was talking about him. Steve Derrick was killed in action. Stella was saddened by the news. Anna said it was God's intervention.

On September 9, 1940, Michael became a father. It was a girl and they named her Sonia after her aunt.

It was just before Christmas that old man Chornoboy became ill. He was elderly in his eighties and was not expected to live very long. Anna and Metro took Stella and Anne to see him and paid their respects. He lay very still on the bed and his eyes were shut. The girls were frightened and did not want to stay there long.

The school was having a play and Mr. Soloway was in charge of the production at the community hall. He also led the choir in the singing of the Christmas Carols. It was during the performance that someone had come backstage and told Olive that her grandfather had passed away.

Again Anna took Stella and Anne to pay their last respects to the old man. It was an eerie feeling for the girls but they stood by the bed and looked at the old man. His face was very white and they had him dressed up in his fancy suit. The priest was there administering the last rights. Many other people came to the house to see him before he was placed in a casket and taken away for burial. It was the first time the girls had ever seen a dead man and they felt very uncomfortable.

Johnny and Bill in Flin Flon

Chapter 31

Trick or Treat

Anna planted her garden again in the spring. Metro's health was not improving and in fact, his feet were really giving him a great deal of trouble. His white hair was still as thick as ever and he did not lose any of it. He was not much help to Anna though. He still read to her during the winter months and she was enjoying the stories from the old country.

Anna received a letter from the family in Flin Flon. It was a sobering letter. They advised that Fred had been drafted and had passed his physical. They said that he was in the army now and was stationed somewhere in Winnipeg. Anna was devastated. Later that same month Fred arrived on leave. He was sharp looking in his army uniform. Anna was frightened. She thought about him going to war and getting shot.

One day when Fred was out, Anna went through his duffle bag and found a small package. She immediately knew what was in the package and was very upset at Fred about it. When Fred returned, she confronted him with the prophylactic. She scolded him for his lack of morals. He assured her that he did not use the prophylactic, that it was part of the army issuance. They were automatically issued to every soldier, he tried to convince her. Anna refused to listen and threw the package in the stove.

Shortly Fred was gone. A few weeks later Anna received a letter from him stating that the army had discharged him because he was an "F". He was not physically fit to be in the armed forces. Somehow the medical team had made an error and discovered Fred might have sugar diabetes. Anna had mixed emotions about the news. She was joyous over the news of his discharge, but saddened about the possible illness of Fred with sugar diabetes. In any event, Fred would not be going to war and getting shot at.

It all happened so suddenly. One day Anna received another letter from the children. They had rented this house and it was large enough to accommodate everyone, they wrote. They had been through a lot when they were small and they wanted something better for the younger children. They wanted Anna and Metro to give up their place and move to Flin Flon. It was the best thing for them they said to have the children all together again. The two girls could finish their school year in the big town and would be better off for it. They needed Anna and her help with the cooking and generally looking after the household.

Anna was in a turmoil. What should she do she wondered. She would dearly love to be with all her children again. She was 53 years old and was not getting any younger. She would have to give up her church. She wondered if there would be a Ukrainian church in Flin Flon. Not likely, Metro said. On the other hand it would be nice to have all the children with her again just like on the old homestead. Besides, she would not have to worry about money any more. Metro wrote back and advised the children that Anna had agreed to the move. The children would be sending the tickets by return mail. Anne and Stella were excited. They bragged about it at school and all their friends were sad about the news.

Anna went to some of her neighbours and advised them to help themselves to her vegetable garden. She also bartered the chickens and turkeys for some clothing and shoes. The few precious possessions she had, she packed in the old trunk and took with her. Mostly, it was the feather tick and pillows. The furniture remained in the house. It consisted of a bed, Metro's cot and the table and chairs. She could not sell the stove, so she left it where it was. They closed the door behind them and proceeded to the train depot.

It was a joyous reunion upon their arrival in Flin Flon. The house was not large but it was sufficient to lodge the entire family. Anne and Stella started school immediately and were soon making new friends. Peter was going to school as well and was a changed person from the son Anna had been having so much trouble with in Fork River.

Andrew was still single and had no girlfriend that he was involved with. Fred was thinking of moving to Ontario. He had heard so much about the city of Hamilton and was contemplating very seriously quitting his job and taking the next train out to Hamilton. On week ends, he would take Peter with him on his runs delivering bread. Peter wanted to quit school and work for Mr. Flocks too.

Anna was confused. Everyone was working during the day and she did the cooking for their evening meal. But she was not happy. She missed her church and her friends. She also yearned for her old place. She especially missed her garden. There was no garden to be had in this town. It was all rocks. The only thing growing on these rocks were blueberries. Metro had no newspaper to read and he also longed for the old days. Anna had no chickens to save feathers for her ticks and pillows, so her fingers were idle for a change. With no garden or chickens to raise, and no church to go to, Anna became very depressed at times.

One day Fred took off for Hamilton, Ontario. Later he wrote to the family and advised them of the beauty of this city. He was working for the steel company and making more money than he had ever dreamed of. He wrote about walking down the street, picking the fruit off the trees and eating it. It sounded so much like paradise, no one could imagine how wonderful this city really was.

Anna decided one day that she wanted to make some blueberry jam. She had heard so much about the blueberries from Andrew and how plentiful they were around his shack. She wanted to get busy doing the things she was used to doing. Like making jam for the winter months. Old habits never die.

So it was that Anna, Pauline and Stella took off to pick blueberries across the lake. Andrew told them they could sleep in his shack because he would be away for a few days. So they were ferried across by boat to the other side of the lake. They then had to walk about two miles to get to the shack. It was a lonesome walk along the railway tracks. Nothing but rocks and bush.

They began picking blueberries and Stella was frightened of bears. Andrew warned them that a bear was rummaging around the shack at night looking for food. There were so many berries that they filled up an aluminum tub full that day. They managed to get it to the shack just before nightfall.

As they were preparing their evening meal by the light of the coal oil lamp, they heard noises outside. An animal was out there and they could hear it coming around to the front of the shack, thrashing through the bushes. It was a big animal and it had to be a bear. They were all extremely frightened. Andrew had a large 12 by 12 beam in the shack just for this purpose. Between the three of them, they managed to prop the beam up against the door, in case the bear should come to the door of the shack. It was a scary night for all of them. The next day they carried the tub of blueberries down the tracks to the man with the ferry boat. Stella was never so glad to get back to the mainland. Anna made her blueberry jam and was pleased about the trip.

Stella was only eleven years old but she was mature enough to baby sit for Michael and his wife. It was her first experience as a baby sitter and she loved it. They paid her for baby sitting and she thought how wonderful it was to make some money too.

It was their first Halloween too. Anne and Stella had never heard of Halloween before. It was quite an event for them. The other children at school briefed them as to what to expect. They took two sacks with them, one for each of them and knocked on all the doors until their sacks were almost full. They would return home and get another sack and go out again and repeat the routine. They received all sorts of apples, cookies, chocolate and candy. Stella had never in her eleven years seen such a horde of goodies. Anna let them eat their loot as much as they wanted to, and there was enough left over for the rest of the family.

That winter, a public skating rink was erected just across the road from the house Anna's family was living in. The boys had purchased a pair of skates for Anne and Stella and they would go out and skate on the rink every evening. They learned to skate quite well and spent most of their spare time at the rink. They were so close to the house that they didn't bother to take off their skates but instead merely went back and forth to the house with their skates on.

The girls would sometimes go to the movies. Johnny and Bill would let them get in for nothing. It was during the matinee. One time in particular, the movie "Snow White and the Seven Dwarfs" was playing. The girls were in awe. It was the first Walt Disney movie they had ever seen and they sat through it twice.

That winter, the older girls decided they would like to go to Hamilton too. They quit singing on the radio and were making plans for their move. Fred had been writing to them about the place so much that they could stand the suspense no longer. Anna suspected that Fred was lonely and was encouraging the family to go to Hamilton. Pauline, Jessie and Sonia took the train out of Flin Flon to Hamilton, Ontario.

Anna was very unhappy. This town was nothing more than a mining town with lots of rocks. She did not want to stay in Flin Flon without the girls. Her family was split up again. She decided that come spring she was moving back to Fork River where she belonged.

The following spring Anna, Metro and the two young girls also took the train back to Fork River as Anna had planned. They could not move into her old place because it had deteriorated so much being unoccupied for over a year. So they moved in with Mary on the farm.

The girls had to walk from the farm to Fork River to go to school. Meanwhile, Anna prepared the old place to make it habitable for her family to move back in.

Anna and Stella Picking Blue Berries

Chapter 32

Meanwhile, Back on the Farm

It was difficult having two women in one household for Anna. She was used to running the whole show even in Flin Flon, she was in control. Here, of course, Mary was in charge because it was her home not Anna's. They tried to get along and Anna would sometimes tell Mary to do things her way. Mary would object and would remind Anna that this was her house. Anna kept busy going back and forth to the house in Fork River fixing up her old place.

There was an election coming up. Mary and Anna would discuss politics on a daily basis. There was an air of expectancy everywhere as to who would vote for which party. Anna insisted that she would be voting Liberal, mainly because she believed the CCF party was communist and so was the third party. Mary tried to convince Anna that this was not the case but she could not influence her.

Anna found the old stove in her house to still be in operational condition. The pyatz was broken in places and Anna had to patch it up. It was too late to plant the garden. Besides, Anna did not have anyone to work up the soil, so she gave up the idea of a garden for that spring. The weeds were so bad that it would have taken Anna a week of hoeing to get rid of them. Everything was really rundown and Anna worked hard to get it back into shape for occupancy.

Stella and Anne were enjoying school and having their old friends back. They had more clothing than they had before their move to Flin Flon and this gave them a sense of self worth.

Mary had a small stainless steel bank at home. She would save all her extra change in it. One day she discovered it was broken into and some money was missing from it. She immediately went to Anna and told her that she thought Stella had broken into her bank. When Stella arrived home from school, they confronted her with the busted bank. Anne was not home as yet. Stella denied it was her and was very frightened. Anna was prepared with the strap ready for the punishment. Stella had seen her sister Anne with some candy at school that day and knew that it had to be her little sister who had stolen the money. So in desperation, she mentioned this to her mother and Mary. Mary still insisted that it was Stella who took the change. When Anne got home from school shortly thereafter, she could not deny the fact that it was she who had taken the money. Mary was very surprised and said she still thought it was Stella who was the thief. Stella looked dumbfounded and bewildered at her older sister.

Anna gave her young daughter a good licking but it hurt her more than it did Anne. She did not like to punish her little baby and Anna was depressed about the beating. She blamed Mary and resented her for it.

Not long after the incident, the four of them moved back to Fork River and Anna was happy to be in charge of her own household again. She purchased some chickens and started on another pillow. Anna and Metro also had the church to go to again. Metro did not have his newspaper to read but was making plans on receiving it again. The girls were happy not to have to walk to the farm everyday to and from school. Everything seemed to be working out for all of them.

It was like the calm before the storm. No sooner were they settled, then they received a letter from the girls in Hamilton. Johnny, Bill and Peter had joined the three girls and Fred in Hamilton. The boys had quit their jobs in Flin Flon and were now working in Hamilton, Ontario.

Pauline, Jessie and Sonia were working in a textile factory. Johnny was employed by a company that manufactured socks. Bill was hired by Dofasco and was working shifts. Peter had quit school and was doing odd jobs. He was also very interested in cars. Fred, of course, was still working for the steel company. He had met this girl by the name of Mary and was quite serious about her. This left only Michael and Andrew in Flin Flon. Michael wrote and advised that Andrew had quit his job on the railway and had again joined Michael working in the bush cutting wood. One night as they were sitting around the fire, the others at the bush camp began to drink quite heavily and they dared Andrew to join them. Andrew, who did not drink, finally took them up on the dare. Apparently, he got quite drunk that night and it was the start of a new era for him. He was putting away a couple of cases of beer everyday not to mention the hard stuff. It was affecting his performance at work. Anna was very disappointed with her son when she heard this. He had lived so long without liquor. He was 27 years old. Why would he start drinking now and over a silly dare, Anna pondered.

Shortly, the girls wrote again and said that Pauline and Jessie had both fallen in love with two wonderful guys and were planning on having a double wedding. They had met their boyfriends at a dance in the hall under the Ukrainian church one Sunday night. They sent pictures of their men together with them and everyone was in awe. The men were both so dark and handsome! The girls were both blonde and very pretty. They looked so beautiful together. Stella and Anne took the pictures to school. Once again they bragged to their friends about their future brothers-in-law. Pauline and Jessie wanted the family to attend their wedding. They got together and managed to accumulate enough money to send to Anna for their fare to Hamilton. Once more Anna's life was disrupted, but she was anxious to be at her daughters' weddings.

So it was that Anna once more packed her meagre belongings into the trunk and the four of them took the train out of Fork River. It was July, 1942. Anna said goodbye to her place again for the last time. She knew she would not be returning. She merely closed the door on the little house she called home for over five years and turned her back on it. They were headed for a far better life in this big city she called paradise.

Pauline and Jessie

Chapter 33

Off to the Big City

They were all living in a three-storey house with a young couple who rented out the upper two floors to the family. It was close to the steel company. Fred had apparently obtained a room there for himself when he first arrived in the city. When the girls joined him, they were also given rooms in the same house. Subsequently, the three boys also moved in and now Anna, Metro and the two youngsters were there also. It was crowded but the landlady was very nice and was happy to see the whole family together. She let them have the run of the house including the kitchen.

The first Sunday of their arrival, the girls planned on a picnic. The two handsome beaus of Pauline and Jessie were also there. They both had cars and they packed everyone into the two cars except Johnny, Bill and Peter. The girls made up a picnic hamper filled with food, and they prepared to take off for the park. They took along their guitars as well, together with a case of beer.

They were arguing as to what car Anne would ride in. They all wanted to have Anne in their car. In all the confusion, they forgot about Stella and went off without her. She stayed at home and looked out the window watching them drive off. She became very paranoid. Johnny came home shortly after that and scolded her for not going with the others. Stella told him that they did not want her with them and began to cry. They had been to the park, had taken pictures, ate and drank beer and everyone enjoyed themselves.

The double wedding was to be on August first. Pauline was all set but Jessie was crying upstairs in her room. Something was wrong and Anna was upset. Jessie and her boyfriend were whispering. They would not talk about it with the others. It was suggested that Steve did not want to get married. Eventually it was decided that Jessie would not be getting married on the same day as Pauline. Jessie cried and Stella felt so sorry for her that she cried too.

Stella found a clean dress but it required ironing. She had watched her sisters use the iron and plugged it in the wall. She proceeded to iron her dress on the floor. When she left for the wedding, she also left the iron plugged in and facing down on the wooden floor. Later, the landlady smelled something burning and on checking, found the iron plugged in and scorching the floor. Needless to say, she was very upset.

Anna was very proud of her daughter Pauline. She was dressed in a long white gown and she looked beautiful. Sonia was one of the bridesmaids. Fred and Johnny were also part of the wedding party. The wedding was not a large one but they had rented a hall for it. They had music, they danced and the wedding guests had supper after that. It was a successful and happy time for everyone.

A week later, Jessie and her boyfriend Steve got married and Anna was so happy for Jessie. It had made her sad to see Jessie cry but Jessie was smiling now and made a beautiful bride also.

The house they lived in was just too crowded. At Anna's insistence, the boys decided that they would lease a house for the entire family. Bill and Johnny rented a house on the next street over and then charged the others a monthly rate to help pay for the rent. Jessie and Steve moved into a small apartment of their own. Pauline and her husband decided to move in with the rest of the family into their rental premises. They rented a three storey place identical to the other house they were living in previously. It was beside the railway tracks. Anna was familiar with the surroundings by this time and was happy to be in the same area. The district consisted of mostly Italian families and they soon accepted Anna and her family. They went out of their way to make Anna and her brood welcome. Communication was the only problem but Anna somehow managed to make herself understood.

They moved into the house and what a feeling it was to have the entire family together again, for the exception of Michael and Andrew. The house had three bedrooms on the third floor, three bedrooms and a bathroom on the second floor and a living room, dining room and kitchen on the first floor. They had a problem at first getting the furnishings but eventually the house was furnished sufficiently to meet their needs.

Anna slept in one of the bedrooms on the second floor with Anne. Metro slept on a cot in the living room on the first floor, because of the problem with his legs. Sonia and Stella slept in one of the bedrooms on the third floor. Pauline and her new husband had the big bedroom in the front of the house on the second floor. The other three bedrooms were shared by the four boys. It was spacious and everyone was happy.

Anna found out about the Ukrainian church nearby and started to go to church on Sundays. Metro was not able to walk too far and was content to sit on the veranda and say his rosary. All in all, Anna was happy with the big city. She had her big house again like the old homestead and she had all her family together, just like the old days. She had finally found some happiness and was satisfied with the arrangement.

Pauline and Johnny Sartorio Wedding

Chapter 34

Anna Citified

Later that fall, Fred announced that he was getting married too. Anna had met his fiancé and they did not hit it off very well. His fiancé was Hungarian and could speak Ukrainian but that was not the problem. Fred was upset with Anna and insisted that she did not like his Mary. His feelings were hurt. They argued constantly about it. Finally Fred told Anna that there was nothing she could say that would change his mind. He was getting married whether she liked it or not. They had a fairly big wedding and his bride wore a beautiful white gown. They met her family and they appeared to be very nice people. So Fred was married that fall. He moved out of the house to go and live with his wife's parents not too far from Anna's place.

Anna learned to ride the street car and buses. She would walk to the main street and then hop the street car to go to church. This was quite an experience for her. She also learned to get transfers and was really proud of herself. She had become citified.

She discovered a small corner store a few streets over and did her grocery shopping there on credit. Once a month, she would have them tally up her purchases and she would pay cash for the tab. It was nice to have the money to pay for things, she thought. She was in charge of her household again and the boys left the running of it entirely in her hands. She prepared the meals and was responsible for the household money.

The furnace in the old house was a coal furnace. Anna thought that this was an expensive way to heat the house for the winter. She spotted some wood on the railway tracks. She would go and collect it for firewood. Mostly, it was 2 x 4's. The lady next door was very pleasant and would sometimes help Anna to gather the wood. One day as the train was going by, one of the men spotted Anna with the wood and chased her down the tracks to the house. He warned her that she could be charged with stealing as the wood was the property of the railway company. This, however, did not deter Anna and she continued to collect the wood for the coming winter.

During the winter months, Fred would invite Anna, Metro and the two small girls to have dinner at his in-laws place. They would catch the street car to the street where Fred lived and walk to the house. Metro's feet were bothering him and he could not walk very far. What a lavish dinner they would enjoy. All of his wife's family would attend at dinner as well. Anna never had anything so adequately prepared. There was roast beef, small baked potatoes and gravy, home made dinner rolls, salad and vegetables. For dessert, there was home made apple pie with ice cream. Fred's wife would help her mother with dinner and Fred was very proud of his new bride. Anna guessed Fred was showing off, but she did not refuse his dinner invitations.

Stella and Anne were going to St. Anne's, a Catholic school about a mile away. It was next door to a St. Anne's Catholic church. The girls would ask Anna for a nickel now and then to catch the street car to school. Mostly, they would walk the distance as Anna thought that they were getting too lazy. They would often leave a little early and go to church first before going to school. Anna was pleased about this.

Pauline was expecting a baby. Once a week she would ask the girls to come into her room and listen to the "Shadow Knows". Pauline would put out the lights to make it spooky and then turn on the radio and the girls would be frightened out of their wits listening to the show. However, this did not prevent them from coming back the following week for the next episode.

Anna was surprised at the winter months. There was very little snow and it was mild in comparison to the winters in Manitoba. Spring came early and she had the boys dig up the postage stamp back yard for her and planted her garden. It was nice to have chives and fresh carrots for her chicken soup on Sundays.

That summer Andrew came down for an extended visit. He was drinking a lot and Anna was very unhappy with him. He spent most of his days with a bottle of beer in his hand. Anna could do nothing.

Anna wanted to make some extra money. She heard from the ladies at the church about canning peaches. She and Sonia took off to the town of Jordan one day to the peach factory where they canned peaches. It was about 40 miles away from Hamilton and they had to sleep over at the site where accommodations were provided for migrant workers. Pauline was in charge of the cooking while Anna was away. It was pleasant for the others to savour Pauline's cooking for a change.

Fred and Mary Kuzyk Wedding

Chapter 35

Call to Arms

Andrew packed his cymbali and left for Flin Flon. He did not want to go back to work in the bush. He had written to say that he was interested in a piece of property and there were plans of building a hotel on the border of Saskatchewan and Manitoba on the outskirts of Flin Flon. He would have to acquire a couple of silent partners and the appropriate licenses first so everything was still up in the air.

Jessie and Steve would drop in frequently. Her husband played the guitar too. He would often sing and play Ukrainian songs which Anna would enjoy. She would sometimes join in and sing with him. Everyone liked Steve. He was very musical and he was such a happy go lucky guy.

Fred and his wife would visit as well. Fred would bring his banjo along. He had learned to play it on his own. Pauline and Jessie would also join in on the singing and everyone would have a great time. There was always music in the house and this made Anna very happy. Her children were all talented in that respect.

Fred received a letter from Michael that winter, indicating that he had a contract with a lumber company whereby a great deal of money was to be made. He needed help as Andrew was no longer available. Fred was getting tired of shift work at the steel company anyway, so he talked it over with his wife and decided to go to Flin Flon.

His wife was expecting a baby and was hesitant to let him go. She had her family, Fred insisted and it was only going to be for a short while. As soon as he found a decent place for them to live, he would send for her. His wife finally agreed and they said their goodbyes. A few days after he left, his wife had a miscarriage. She was heartbroken. They really wanted children and this was her second miscarriage. She could not carry after a two month pregnancy the doctor told her.

Sonia was dating a fellow down the street. He seemed like a nice enough guy. He had two brothers who were identical twins. The younger girls had never seen a set of twins in their entire lives. They marvelled at them. Sonia had gone out with this chap a couple of times. One night she came home crying. Her hair and clothing were in disarray. She said the man had tried to force himself upon her and almost raped her. She fought him off and eventually he gave up and let her go. Sonia swore to Anna that he had not touched her. She would not go out with the man again. Every time Anna ran into the guy, she would shake her finger at him in admonishment.

Bill too got tired of working shifts. He quit his job at the factory. He took up body and fender repairs at an automobile company. He enjoyed working on cars. Peter, of course, had already quit school and was working at odd jobs and making a few dollars wherever he could.

One day Jessie's husband Steve received his draft notice. Jessie was in tears. He had his physical and was drafted. Jessie did not want to stay in the apartment by herself. Pauline and her husband had moved in with his mother, so the front room on the second floor was vacant. Pauline had a baby boy and she and her husband were both very happy together. Jessie moved in with the family and Steve would come and visit her on his leave.

The following Spring, Fred's wife advised Anna that she was going to Flin Flon to join her husband. She had quit her job. She was very excited about the prospect of being reunited with Fred again.

Anna made a couple of pies one day and left them on the counter to cool. She came downstairs later in the evening to put them in the ice box. When she switched on the lights, she was flabbergasted. She had never seen so many insects in a house at one time before. The floor appeared to be moving with them. There were cockroaches scurrying about for cover everywhere. They were on the counter, on the floor and on the stove. She also had bread in the bread box and wondered if the roaches were in there too. It was the first time she had noticed the insects and she decided to have a talk with Bill about it.

Anna could always count on Bill. He never doubted or questioned her judgment. The next day Anna told Bill that she wanted to move out of the house. Bill had saved some money for himself and Anna thought that they should buy a house of their own. It was like throwing the money away paying rent every month. Why not put the money towards a house of their very own, she insisted. It made a lot of sense to Bill so he set out to purchase a home.

They found a beautiful big house on an exclusive residential street. It had five bedrooms on the second floor with a bath. The attic was equally as large and if one so desired, it could be modified into a full floor of extra bedrooms. There was an exquisite round stained glass window facing the street in the attic. The house came partially furnished. A side entrance had been built to the kitchen area of the house and what appeared to have been a servant's staircase at one time, led from the kitchen to the upper floor. Presumably, this had been used by the servants as their entrance to the rooms above. The main staircase in the front of the house was circular and it was solid oak. When it was polished, the wood just gleamed. There were several windows of stained glass with intricate designs. A large round stained glass window was situated above the first landing going up the stairs. There were hardwood floors throughout the house.

The main entrance in the front had French doors and they were stained glass too. A second set of French doors led into a massive hallway. The living room was to the left of the entrance leading into a large spacious room with a fireplace. A dining room with French doors was situated next to the living room and a huge parlour was just off the gigantic kitchen. The wainscoting was in pristine condition. In the big back yard there was a cherry tree and it was in full bloom.

The house was old and was originally owned by a wealthy Judge who, it was rumoured, was a cruel and ruthless man. He had been known to torture some of the people he was involved with. Bill purchased the house for $7,000.

Steve Andrusyshen in Uniform

Chapter 36

Bootleg Monkey Business

It was a quiet neighbourhood and Anna was very pleased with the house. Metro would sit on the front porch while saying his rosary. He still had all his hair and it was thick and a silvery white. He was as handsome as he ever was.

Stella was going to high school and Anne was not too far behind. Jessie was working and had moved into one of the larger bedrooms overlooking the back yard paying her share of the rent. She decided that no one was permitted to enter her room in her absence. In the room, Jessie had a beautiful bedspread and matching curtains and a fancy rug on the floor beside the bed. It was a pretty room.

Johnny and Peter shared the large bedroom in the front of the house, and Sonia and Stella occupied the bedroom in the back, near where the cherry tree grew. Bill had a bedroom for himself, and the family gave the remaining bedroom to a cousin from Fork River. Anna slept in the parlour with Anne, after converting the large room into a bedroom. Metro continued to sleep on a cot in that same room.

Anna chose to place in her room a side cupboard that came with the house. It was a very old piece of furniture, and Anna made it her altar. She had placed statues on it, together with a few holy pictures and holy water. The cupboard was presumably an oak piece though this was hard to tell because it had been painted over with a very dark brown stain. It had Queen Anne legs, a small mirror and stained-glass side doors. There were other pieces of furniture about the house which the family utilized, but this one was Anna's special piece.

Anna was very happy with the change in living arrangements. On several occasions, she had switched on the lights in the kitchen at night to check for cockroaches and was relieved to find that there were none. She had her big house again. They had indeed gone far since their homesteading days. She soon familiarized herself with the area and was back to shopping, soon settling down into a very comfortable lifestyle.

Not long after, Anna began bootlegging again. The taverns closed at midnight, and somehow a few people found out that Anna was open for business. These strangers would appear at the side door, and Anna would let them into the kitchen. No one knew how it got started or where they came from.

Pretty soon Anna would be entertaining these people in her kitchen on a regular basis. Since she slept in the parlour just off the kitchen area, she was always readily available. Usually her customers would arrive shortly after midnight. The boys, and in particular Bill, objected strenuously, but to no avail. Anna needed the extra money to help pay for the mortgage.

There were three people in particular who were steady customers a big man in his late forties with two women. They were always a threesome. They would also arrive on Sunday afternoons, which was not appreciated by the family. When they did come at night, Bill would try and reason with Anna that he and the rest of the family had to get up early for work. These people coming in so late disrupted their sleep. They were loud, continually laughed and could be heard upstairs. Anna would hear none of it. Johnny tried to intimidate her by telling her they could all go to jail if Anna got caught. This did not frighten her and she continued to bootleg.

The cherry tree in the back produced beautiful bing cherries. Sonia and Stella would just reach out the window, pick and eat their fill. They were ripe and juicy and they enjoyed them very much.

Steve would come home on leave to see Jessie and they would spend some very emotional times together. Jessie would write to her husband on a daily basis when they were apart. They were very much in love. There were rumours that he might be shipped overseas before too long. This made Anna very concerned about her own sons getting drafted and going to war.

Andrew came home for another extended visit. He had some money saved and was not planning on getting a job in Hamilton. He had purchased a house in Flin Flon. He was renting a large portion of it out and was making good money. He was still drinking heavily. The drinking would start first thing in the morning and continue until late at night. Anna would not allow him to touch her stock of beer. He would go down to the brewery and order a couple of cases of beer at a time. The brewery would deliver the beer to him at the house.

Some weekends Jessie, Peter, Sonia and Bill would play cards together. Mostly it was hearts they played. An argument would break out now and again and Anna would have to intervene. It was always Jessie who would win at cards. She would memorize the cards and what had been played and play her cards accordingly.

All in all, it was a very happy family unit. Anna would still do all the cooking. The girls would help her sometimes and everything ran pretty smoothly. Anna generally made chicken soup for Sunday night dinner and everyone made sure they were home to enjoy it.

Michael wrote and said that he had enough of Flin Flon. It was agreed that his wife Jean and their two small children would be coming to Hamilton to join the family. Michael had some unfinished business to attend to first and would be following her shortly. Fred and his wife planned on staying in Flin Flon. Michael's little girl was just three years old and their son was approximately eight months old.

Anna made preparations for Michael's wife and her two small children. Johnny moved in with Bill. Peter, who had been sharing a room with his cousin was now sharing it with Andrew. The cousin eventually moved out completely and obtained a room elsewhere. They arranged for another bed to be brought up into the big front bedroom upstairs. Jean arrived and they welcomed her into their home. She was very happy with the arrangements and soon settled down to life in the big city.

There was some talk about getting a telephone in the house. Anna was still a bit old fashioned and insisted that it was a luxury they could not afford at the present time.

Sonia, Stella, Anne and Jessie

Chapter 37

Missing Hazelnuts

Shortly, Michael arrived and joined his wife in the front bedroom. He decided that he would go into business for himself. He had done some painting and wallpapering in Flin Flon and was experienced in that field. He started out by doing the wallpapering of one of the neighbours. They liked it very much and soon he had established himself and was working pretty steady.

One day about three months after Michael had arrived, he advised Anna that he would be moving out. He had rented this big house in a working class area. He and his family were going to be moving as soon as possible. His family was growing and they needed more space. Anna did not object and was, in fact, relieved.

Bill had purchased a car. It was the very first car anyone in the family ever had. It was an American model that had been involved in an accident. It was a convertible and Bill fell in love with it. He purchased it for practically nothing and with his knowledge of body and fender work, had fixed it up to look like new. He had already learned how to drive and everyone was very excited about his new car.

During the summer holidays, Anna, Pauline, Sonia, Stella and Anne left for Jordan to can peaches. They were all staying in one room at the site and were making good money. Even Anne who was only thirteen years old was working at the factory. The two younger girls had to come home early because of school, but the others remained until the peach season was over.

In the fall, Bill had gone out and picked a sack full of hazelnuts. He spread them out on a sheet of plywood in the attic to dry and was contemplating on them being dried out by Christmas. Anna too was preparing for the winter. She had learned everything there was to know about the art of making wine from her Italian friends. She ordered several bushel baskets of grapes from a man in her old neighbourhood. She purchased a keg and soon the wine was brewing. The whole family sampled it and were enjoying a glass or two of wine mixed with ginger ale.

Jessie was very upset one week-end. She had received a letter from her husband stating that he was being shipped overseas and would be coming home on leave for his last visit. Everyone tried to console her but she cried constantly. Steve soon arrived and they spent most of their time together in her room. No one talked about his being shipped out in front of them. In the past, whenever he left the house, Steve would just come down the circular staircase, walk right out the front door and not bother to say goodbye to the others. Jessie would never come downstairs to see him off but would remain in her room crying. So on this day Stella busied herself by the staircase when she thought it was his time to leave. Sure enough Steve came down the stairs. Stella was crying and gave him a big hug and said her goodbye.

Winter had arrived and the snow was on the ground. Sonia and Stella thought about the hazelnuts and went up to the attic to investigate to see if the nuts were ready to eat. They brought a big bowl full of them downstairs to their bedroom one night and with a nutcracker, began to sample the nuts. They were ready and very delicious. They began to sample them on a nightly basis and pretty soon by the time Christmas rolled around, they had eaten most of the hazelnuts. One night Bill caught them coming downstairs from the attic with a bowl full of the nuts. He went up to the attic to assess the damage and found to his dismay that there were very few nuts left for the Christmas season. He barged into their room. Both girls were in bed and were very distraught. First he put Stella over his knees and gave her a good sound spanking. Then he did the same with Sonia. Stella was fifteen and Sonia was almost twenty. Neither one of them said a word. They had always looked up to Bill and were very much ashamed. It was so uncharacteristic of him to have done this. Bill told them that if they behaved like small children, they should be treated like small children and he left the room.

The snow started falling in the early evening. It came down heavy and soon everyone was rushing to get home before it became impossible to drive in. The following morning, there was over three feet of snow on the ground. The worst snowfall of the century. There were no tracks of any kind in the snow anywhere and one could not distinguish the roads from the sidewalks.

Stella was happy that she would not have to go to school that day. Her happiness was short lived. Anna insisted that school was open and that Stella better start out because she was already late. Her school was within walking distance. Anne had to take the street car to her school and Anna could see that they were not running. Dejected, Stella got dressed and proceeded out the door. The high school was about six blocks away.

The snow was very deep and it took her an hour to get to the school. Her boots were full of snow. There were no other tracks in the snow anywhere. No one else was foolish enough to venture out into the street. Of course, when Stella finally reached the school, it was closed tight. She retraced her steps and finally reached home. Stella resented her mother for making her walk in the snow that day.

Steve and Jessie Andrusyshen Marriage

Chapter 38

Cherry Picking

Johnny decided he wanted to get a car too. He had saved up some money and was contemplating getting a fancy Buick. He also quit his job at the sock factory and obtained a position at the downtown hotel as a bell hop. He was making good tips, was meeting a lot of interesting people and he enjoyed his new job. In no time, he was promoted to bell captain and Anna was very impressed with Johnny. Johnny was playing the field and dated several girls. Bill was not dating anyone as yet and Anna was content with this arrangement. He was still young and had plenty of time to mess with women.

One day Anna received a letter from the municipality of Mossey River. She marvelled at how they found out where she lived. She in fact, was still paying taxes for the old place in Fork River and this is how they located her. They wanted to buy her place and offered her $700.00 for her property. They were planning on putting a road through her place and to run a bridge across the river past the Lacey's. Anna agreed without any hesitation and went to see a lawyer about the transaction. She had never expected to get any money for the property and this was a pleasant surprise.

Stella got a job working on week-ends at a restaurant in the downtown area and was making some good tips too. She would save her money and put it towards new clothes for herself. She met a young woman who was the cashier for the place. She was a few years older than Stella but they became very good friends. This young woman sort of looked after Stella at the restaurant.

It was Easter time and Anna wanted the entire family to attend services at the Ukrainian church. Bill was also religious and needed no prodding. Stella was decked out in her new outfit which she purchased through the layaway plan. It was a two hour service and everyone was hungry when they got home. Anna had prepared the Easter Sunday dinner. There was plenty of chicken, mashed potatoes and stuffing. Anna had also baked a couple of round loaves of bread with raisins for the occasion and had them blessed at the church.

The cherry tree was in bloom and the girls could hardly wait for the fruit to appear. When the cherries ripened Sonia and Stella picked and ate their fill. They were black and sweet and the girls gobbled them up. At one point Stella was just playing with one of the cherries, when she opened it up and discovered to her horror a big fat worm in it. She made a face and decided to open another cherry and found it too had a fat worm in it. She made Sonia aware of it and pretty soon they discovered that all the cherries had worms in them. The tree had not been sprayed in years and the girls did not realize that this was a necessary function. Needless to say, they did not eat any more cherries after that.

Peter had turned 19 years old that May and he received notification from the army. He too was drafted after getting his physical. Anna was reassured by the others that it was the best thing that could happen to Peter. The army would make a man out of him. If nothing else, it would straighten him out.

Stella turned sixteen years old that August 1945. She had a birthday party and invited all her friends from school over that evening. Bill attended the party and they played spin the bottle and everyone had a good time. Anna had purchased a birthday cake for the occasion and Stella was very pleased.

Metro was having nightmares. Anna talked to Bill about his problem. He was seeing things. She thought that it was the evil spirit of the judge that was roaming about the house. Metro would be frightened and could not sleep at night she told Bill. She was very concerned about him and decided to pour wax over his head. She was convinced that the trouble lay with the evil spirits in the house. The house was haunted and they should move out. In a way Bill was greatly relieved. Perhaps it would mean the end of Anna's bootlegging. Bill detested that aspect of it. It was summer time and the girls were on summer vacation. It would be a good time to make the move. Anna finally persuaded Bill to sell the place and Bill sold it for $14,000, doubling his money on the transaction.

Anna decided that they should purchase this corner property in the east end of the city. It was a small general store with living quarters in the back. It also had a separate 3 room building at the back of the property. At one time it had been a storage shed and had been modified into a self-contained apartment. The house itself was not very large, but then there was only Johnny, Bill, Sonia, Stella and Anne at home now so they did not require a big place. Jessie could move into the building in the back and she could work for Bill at the store. Anna talked Bill into buying the place and so they once again made the move to yet another place and a business venture.

Peter Kuzyk in Uniform

Chapter 39

Calling All Children

Anna talked Jessie into quitting her job and working in the store for Bill. Jessie was happy to do this in one way. She moved into the building in the back, painted and wallpapered the place to her satisfaction. She was delighted with the results. There was a small bedroom, an equally small living room and a tiny kitchen. It had a two piece bath with a shower and Jessie was in her own little home. It was heated with electrical baseboard heaters. It would be close for her to go to work every morning and no more buses or street cars to ride. This arrangement suited her just fine. Bill paid Jessie a weekly salary. They had an agreement with regard to the living accommodations as well. Bill still worked at his automobile company so he did not worry about the store. He knew it was in good hands. The regular clientele would still cater to the store and business was not too bad, he concluded.

Anna was back to improving the place. She hired a carpenter to come down and extend the living room quarters facing Jessie's place and he enlarged it. He built windows all around the extension and Anna was pleased with the outcome.

Stella was graduating this year and had purchased some white Italian lace material and taken it to a seamstress to make her a dress for graduation. Stella was the first one in Anna's family to graduate from high school. Anna bought Stella a Bulova wrist watch for the occasion and Stella was very happy with it. It was her first piece of jewellery.

Bill and Stella joined the Catholic Youth Organization at the Ukrainian church and were both very active members. The others in the family were not interested in joining the CYO. They met a lot of young people and were soon travelling to the outlying areas at dances and meeting other young people at other CYO's.

At times there would be a week-end affair and they would be put up for the night by the other members from the host city. Bill would act as chaperon for Stella and always looked after her welfare. Stella would appreciate her big brother for his caring ways. It was very exciting. Bill would drive them in his convertible and he was quite happy with all his new friends.

Stella was still working for the restaurant on week-ends but as soon as she graduated, she would have to give it up for a permanent job. Graduation came around for Stella and she asked one of the boys from the CYO to be her escort at the occasion. He was very pleased to be asked. Stella looked stunning in her new long white lace gown. Her dress was the prettiest of all and Anna was very proud once more. Later they had Stella's friend from the restaurant and her husband join them as chaperons for the dance. They had a car and drove them to the dance and home again. All in all it was a perfect evening.

Anna decided with Johnny's prodding that it was time they had a telephone. There was a telephone in the store already and they needed one in the house too he insisted. Anna agreed and the telephone was installed. It was quite an experience for everyone to be able to just pick up the phone and dial anyone they wished. They considered it a real luxury. Jessie too had a telephone installed in her place and everyone was happy.

Just like that suddenly the war was over. Jessie was joyous. She had received a letter from Steve indicating that he was not sure when he would be arriving home. He wrote that the service was shipping them back home gradually and that Jessie should check with the local newspaper to see if his name would appear in the paper as being part of the next regiment out. Jessie checked the newspaper every day looking for his name.

Peter, of course, received his discharge almost immediately as he was not out of the country. He moved back into the house with the family and soon obtained a job at another automobile company fixing cars like Bill.

Metro seemed to be improving. He was not getting any more nightmares and Anna was glad about the move. There was no porch or veranda for him to sit out on so he was content to sit in the armchair in the living room and look out the windows that were installed in the extended area. He never complained about anything.

Anna got more involved with the church. She was aching for the glory days in Fork River and their new church there. She attended a church picnic one day just outside Hamilton. It was held on several acres of land and the church owned this property. The congregation would gather and everyone would bring their own food. Mass would be said outdoors later and everyone would have a great time.

Anna decided that a church should be built on these premises. The land was already there and paid for. She set out to speak to the local priest about it. He ho-hummed the idea and Anna was very disappointed. At her persistence, he agreed that she could buy a couple of plaques and they would be blessed and placed at the site in her name. This she did and the plaques were inscribed in her honour.

The CYO was holding a popularity contest and tickets had been printed for the big event the following fall. Six girls were chosen from the CYO to participate in the contest. Their pictures were printed on the tickets. Each girl received a number of books of tickets and the one who sold the most would win the popularity contest. Stella was one of the girls whose picture was on the tickets. She put her heart and soul into the project and was selling the tickets very rapidly. Anna purchased a number of books herself. They had over six months to go so Stella had plenty of time to sell all her tickets.

Finally, Jessie found Steve's name in the Hamilton Spectator. He was due back home in a couple of days. Everyone was overjoyed for her. He would be arriving about 2:00 a.m. at the Hamilton Armories. This was a process they arranged for the boys coming back from overseas. They would arrive by train then they were bussed to the Armories where their families could then greet them. The Armories was a huge area and could accommodate a lot of people.

Jessie and Stella went to meet Steve at the Armories. The soldiers streamed out of the bussing area in the back and into the building one by one. Jessie spotted her husband immediately. He appeared a little older and somewhat tired but it was still her Steve. She was in his arms and they embraced long and hard. It was good to see them together again. Stella smiled happily as she watched Jessie cry with joy. Steve finally gave Stella a hug and a kiss too. They boarded the street car and then transferred onto a bus to get home. It was a long and tedious trip but they were home at long last. Jessie had her beloved one with her for good. Everyone was very happy for her.

That summer Stella decided to go to the tobacco farms and really make some money. She and Anne boarded the bus and took off for Simcoe and the tobacco country. They were picked up by a farmer and taken to Aylmer where this man was renting his farm. Anne and Stella soon learned how to hand leaves and became very proficient at it. They were making $9.00 per day and this was a great deal of money for them. They both enjoyed the experience and ate well too. The farmer and his wife liked the girls and later asked them if they would return the following year. The girls agreed to keep in touch and they did.

Stella Kuzyk Graduation

Chapter 40

Popularity Contest

Stella and Anne made over $400.00 each working on the tobacco farms. Anna let them keep their hard earned money. Anne put her money in the bank and Stella bought some new clothes with hers. Stella needed some new clothes as she had to look for employment. She got a job working at Eaton's Knitting Mill. She was a stenographer and made $12.50 a week. She could type and take shorthand as she took the business course at the high school. She paid her room and board as everyone had to pay their fair share of the rent to Bill. Her share was $5.00 a week. This was a lot of money to Stella, but everyone had to pay Anna concluded. So Stella did not object.

While at the Catholic high school, the nuns had the classroom do some typing and office work for the local priest and Stella met this priest at the school. He singled her out to do some office work in the church on occasion. She was quite pleased to be chosen and glad to have the experience. He was a tall man, very handsome and Stella respected him as a priest and nothing more.

The Ukrainian church still had regular Sunday night dances and the family would go to these dances every Sunday night. Bill, Sonia, Johnny, Peter and Stella, of course, was now permitted to attend also. She had been forbidden to date as long as she was still at school. The boys took the girls to the dance and also made sure that they got back home with them. Like their mother they all loved to dance.

One such Sunday evening while they were at the dance, the priest from the school came down to the house and questioned Anna about

Stella. Anna told him that Stella was at the dance and he asked her where. She told him where the dance was held. The priest actually came down to the hall. He inquired for Stella at the entrance and there was a commotion at the door. Someone interrupted Stella as she was dancing and told her to come to see this man. She was dumbfounded. What did he want with her? She was confused and flustered when she spoke to him. The priest asked her if she would be planning on staying on at the dance. She told him that she did, quickly excused herself and disappeared in the crowd. She was very embarrassed for him. Anna was astounded when she found out that the priest actually went to the dance to see Stella. She could not believe it. She cautioned Stella but she did not need to fret about it as Stella wanted no part of this situation.

One evening about a week after the dance incident, the priest arrived at the house again. Stella was upstairs and was not aware of him being at the house. He said he wanted Stella to do some typing for him but Anna did not believe him. She told him that Stella was ill and in bed and was not available. He insisted on going upstairs to see her if she was ailing. Anna was shocked, but she remained adamant and told him that he could not go upstairs. She finally managed to discourage him and he went away. Stella hoped that this would end the matter and it did. Later Bill found out that the car he was fixing belonged to the same priest and he said that he found all sorts of bobby pins in the back seat of the vehicle. Bill was very religious and would not normally speak of clergy in this manner so this was an exception for him.

Steve got a job in a hotel a short distance from the house. He would catch the bus to and from work. He was a bartender and he enjoyed his work. Jessie was pregnant and was expecting a baby the following May. She was radiant. She was also very worried. He did not like to drive a car as this is what he mostly did in the army. He drove the big brass in the jeep all over the front lines. It was just as well as far as Jessie was concerned because she did not want him drinking and driving.

The day of the popularity contest had arrived. A huge crowd gathered at the hall. Bill and a few of the other men were in charge of the committee counting up the sale of the tickets. They were almost ready to make the announcement. Stella was dressed in her graduation gown and the other girls were also dressed in long gowns too. They waited in anticipation. The hall was crowded with people on this Sunday afternoon. It was supposed to have been held outdoors at the Ancaster grounds but it was pouring rain and had to be held indoors.

The announcement came. The sales were recorded from the last to the first and Stella won the contest. She had the most ticket returns. Some of the other girls had tickets out but not turned in. Stella was ecstatic. They had little flower girls all dressed up in waiting for Stella and presented her with flowers. A local politician presented her with a clock radio for first prize. Stella was also presented with a large cup with an inscription on it. A space had been left vacant for the name of the winner. She was told her name would be inscribed on the cup and presented to her at a later date. They placed a crown on her head as Queen of the day and it was all very flattering. Anna was, of course, again very proud and strutted about the hall like a peacock. There were pictures taken from every angle and later there was a dance as usual on Sunday night. Most of the older crowd had left and the younger crowd stayed for the dance. Stella was very popular that night as every man wanted a chance to dance with her.

That winter Jessie came to talk to Bill. She was getting pretty large and would not be able to continue much longer working at the store. She was seven months pregnant and gave him a month's notice. Anna was very concerned about the situation. Bill needed someone to work in the store. It was obvious that Jessie would not be able to do it much longer. Stella overheard the discussions. She finally told Bill that she would quit her job and work in the store for nothing. She was not happy with her job at the mill. She had saved herself some money and did not need any more clothes either. She made a point to tell him that this would, of course, include her room and board. Bill agreed and was very grateful to Stella for her kind offer.

Sonia was getting restless and decided to move out one day. She wanted more privacy and rented a room in a big house in the downtown area. She became very friendly with the landlady and they would go to night clubs and dances together.

One day Anne had done something that offended Anna. She was very upset with her. She took out the strap and cornered Anne in the bedroom. Anne was in tears and Stella happened to come in on the scene. She immediately placed herself between Anne and her mother. She told Anna that they were all too big to be getting lickings any more. If Anna wanted to hit anyone she had better start with her. Anna was stunned. This was the first time Stella had ever been so confrontational. Anna hit Stella once then dropped her hand instantly and walked away. That was the last time she ever took the strap out to anyone.

Stella Kuzyk 1945

Chapter 41

Romance Blooms

Johnny bought himself a black Oldsmobile. He acquired a small steel statue of a horse and had it installed on the front of the hood. Soon everyone associated Johnny with the horse and knew it was Johnny's car. He was very proud of his new automobile. Johnny had many girlfriends and was very popular with the ladies. He was very handsome. Johnny was not ready for marriage and usually the women he was involved with had wedding bells on their minds. Johnny would soon break up with them and go into another relationship.

It was Easter time and Anna was preparing for the church services. Afterwards, everyone was invited over to Michael's place for dinner. Michael was leasing a big three bedroom house. He rented out one room to a man and was getting a weekly rate for the room to help in paying the monthly rent for the house. He was also doing very well with the painting and wallpapering business. He and his wife now had three children and everything seemed to be going well for them.

Pauline and her husband, Jessie and Steve, Bill, Sonia, Peter, Stella and Anne came over to Michael's. Anna and Metro were there as well. The family brought their instruments and Michael played his violin. The girls sang and played their guitars and Steve also sang and played the guitar. Everyone had a great time. Metro would just sit and watch and was enjoying all the music. Anna would beam with delight. It was wonderful to be together on this special occasion. They agreed to meet again at Christmas time.

Stella started to work in the store. Jessie helped her out a lot by advising her what to re-order and what not to and pretty soon Stella was running the store without any problems. There was a lady who regularly did her shopping at the store. She had four grown children still at home and needed a great deal of groceries. She would spend approximately $30.00 every week. That was a big order for the store. She was the store's best customer. Her sons would come in and buy cigarettes. A package of cigarettes was $.33. Business was good and Anna was pleased. She too would buy her groceries for the family at the store and Bill was content with the way things were going. Everyone was crazy about orange popsicles. Jessie had a craving for them and would be buying them constantly. Even Anna took a liking to them. Stella was having a problem keeping them in stock. It was something new and the popsicles were five cents each.

Anna received a letter from Andrew. They were starting to build the hotel. All the necessary licenses had been obtained and the hotel would be in Creighton, Saskatchewan. It was the extension of Flin Flon. He had also acquired a couple of silent partners and things were looking good. He would be moving into one of the rooms in the hotel and would rent his house out entirely. Anna was still worried about Andrew's drinking.

Jessie and Steve had become parents. Jessie had a baby girl. She was born on May 12, 1947. Jessie asked Stella to be the Godmother. Stella was very pleased and they baptized her at the Ukrainian church. Anna was again a grandmother.

The store started to slow down that summer. Stella was getting impatient too. She wanted to go to the tobacco farms again and she did not know what to do about the store. She spoke to Bill about it and he was concerned as well. He talked it over with Anna and they decided that it would be in the best interests of everyone if he sold the store. Anna wanted Bill to buy a house close to the church for Metro to be able to attend church regularly. So it was decided that they would look for something about four or five blocks away from the Ukrainian church.

Sonia, Stella and Anne took the bus out of Hamilton to the tobacco farms. They went to the same farmer they had worked for the previous year. He had purchased a farm of his own now and it was situated in Simcoe. He had written and advised the girls that he wanted them back again for the coming season.

Bill had already sold the store and plans were being made to purchase the house on Clinton Street. It was a 30 day closing so Bill was sort of rushed but he knew it was for the best. The store had become a headache he did not need.

Jessie and Steve and their new baby, of course, were forced to do something as well. They would have to move too. They purchased a small house on a street close to the hotel Steve was working at. It was a block away and this made Steve very happy. He could walk to work and home without having to take public transportation.

The girls were making more money than the previous year on the tobacco farm. They were getting $11.00 a day. They were feeling a lot better about it this year too because they knew the man they were working for. It was Sonia's first year though but she learned how to hand the leaves pretty quickly and was soon as good as the other two girls. She started to practise tying tobacco and thought that she would like to do this the following year.

One day while the girls were waiting for the next boat of tobacco to arrive from the field Anne thought she would try her hand at riding the horse. She mounted the animal and the horse started to trot. She was bareback and slowly started to slip off the animal towards the rear end. Stella was petrified. She could see Anne being kicked by the hoofs of the horse as she slipped off and Stella screamed. Anne was off and on the ground. She was not hurt and laughed at Stella's concern, but she did not try to ride the horse again.

Stella met a young man working for the farmer by the name of Willie. He was the farmer's top man and was in charge of the workers in the field. He worked for the farmer during the winter months as well and into spring in the greenhouse transplanting the tobacco plants. Stella and the young man became acquainted and were soon in love. She was going to be eighteen that August and was very young. The boyfriend was twenty-five. Sonia and Anne teased her about the man but Stella was stubborn and insisted that she was in love.

The boyfriend proposed to her and they became engaged. Everything happened so quickly. The farmer's wife was making bets about when they would have children. She predicted within a year. They were the talk of the tobacco farm. Stella did not have a ring as yet but her boyfriend said they would go to Toronto after the harvest to meet his family and purchase the ring at that time.

Bill and Anna moved into their residence while the girls were away. It was an old house beside a warehouse. The train tracks were immediately behind the house just the other side of the wooden fence. It was not a very pretty location. The house had three bedrooms upstairs and a bath. The downstairs had a living room, dining room and kitchen. Nothing special, but it was close to the church and Metro could shuffle back and forth to the church without any problem. Again, he had a porch to sit out on and say his rosary. He was happy with the new house. It did not take much to make Metro happy. The girls had not yet seen the old house and were in for a surprise.

Anne and Anna

Chapter 42

Rushing Bride

The girls got back from tobacco farms with a great deal of money. Sonia decided to stay with the family and she was welcomed home. She did not look for a job immediately. She had met this young man who was barely eighteen years of age and got herself engaged to him.

Stella set out to look for a job. She obtained one at the steel company office and was making good money as a stenographer. Anne still had a couple of years of high school to complete. She had plans to go to college and Anna was very proud of her.

One day Anna hung out her clothes on the clothes line. She had just finished hanging them when a train came by and chugged along the tracks. Anna just stood there and watched as her clean white sheets became blackened with soot from the train. Anna had to take her clothes off the line again and rewash them. Later she had it figured out when the train came by and would hang out her clothes accordingly.

Anna was shocked to find that Stella and Sonia were engaged in such a short time. She had met both boys and could see nothing wonderful about either of them. She told Sonia her boyfriend was too young and she told Stella hers was too old. Stella had finally received her ring. She had gone to Toronto with her boyfriend and he had purchased the engagement ring. Her boyfriend also bought her a cedar chest. Stella felt very important. They had set a date for May 8th the following year as their wedding day. Stella could hardly wait to get out on her own.

Stella's boyfriend continued to remain on the farm and would come to see Stella every week-end. He had a '36 Ford which he seemed to constantly be filling up with oil. He kept two or three gallons of oil in the car at all times for emergency use. He would often have to stop on the highway for a refill of oil.

Suddenly Sonia's boyfriend broke up with her. She was devastated. He just told her that he was not ready to get married as yet. He did not ask for his ring back though. Sonia would mope about the house and was very depressed. She finally moved out of the house again and went back with her previous landlady. They commenced to go to dances and night clubs again.

Stella was preparing for her wedding. She had picked out the four bridesmaids and had sent out all the invitations. She had rented the hall under the church and obtained the services of the women from the church who would be doing the cooking. She was well organized. The priest almost ruined the whole wedding. He suddenly advised one day that the hall might not be available for the date set for the wedding, and asked Stella if she could postpone the wedding a couple of weeks. Stella was constantly in tears. Nothing was going right for her.

Anna thought that Stella was pregnant and was in a rush to get married. All her invitations had been sent out she tried to explain and she could not now advise everyone that the wedding date had been postponed. The priest finally confirmed that the hall was going to be available for the agreed upon date. Stella was relieved. The day of the wedding arrived and Stella was very sad for some reason. She had been through so much turmoil. Her boyfriend was still working on the farm and was not always there for her and she had to run the whole show by herself. She was exhausted on her wedding day. Fred and his wife returned from Flin Flon and decided they would stay in Hamilton. They came to the wedding and Stella was so happy to see them. She cried all the while during the reception. They were not tears of joy, but rather tears of exhaustion.

All in all, the wedding did not go very well. Stella and her new husband stayed at the hotel that night. The next morning she returned to the house to collect her luggage. A lot of the guests were there for another meal. It was the custom for some of the very close family and friends to come over the following day and have another meal from the food left over from the wedding. Stella and her husband finally took off in their '36 Ford up north for their honeymoon. They subsequently moved in with her new husband's father in Toronto where Stella got a job at a flour mill company and her new husband obtained a job with a fire extinguisher firm.

William Duschl and Stella Kuzyk Wedding

Chapter 43

Family Reunion

Fred and his wife still wanted children. She had several more miscarriages in Flin Flon. Fred took her to see a specialist and she was put on some special medication. The doctor told her that she could not carry past the two month period. He told her that these pills she was on would possibly remedy the situation. They were willing to try anything. His wife had thought about adopting a child but Fred was not going for that at all. He wanted his very own child and not someone else's. He told his wife that if they could not have one of their own, he did not want any at all.

They bought a place on Main Street and moved in shortly after that. It was on a very busy street. Fred decided that he would go into business for himself. He had accumulated quite a bit of money in Flin Flon and set himself up in the aluminum screen doors and windows installations business. He placed his business sign out in front of his house. He was doing quite well and his wife was very proud of her husband. They got along exceedingly well.

Stella was expecting a baby. She had worked until the end of her 8th month of pregnancy. She was not very happy in Toronto and she managed to talk her husband into buying a place in Hamilton. Stella missed her family and wanted to be close to them. She felt a need especially in her condition to be near her own family. They purchased a small two bedroom bungalow about six blocks from Anna's place. Her husband obtained a job with a steel company and Stella was content. She would walk the six blocks to see her mother and everything was going well.

Stella gave birth to a little girl a day before their first anniversary. Stella named her Adele. She was born on May 7th, 1949. The night Stella brought her little girl home from the hospital she was having awful nightmares. She could not move and knew she was in bed and she tried to wake herself up. She would start breathing really hard and loud and her husband would touch her and wake her up. Just his contact would be sufficient to bring her out of it. But she would immediately lapse right back into the nightmare.

Adele was in a crib beside her bed. The devil himself was standing over the crib and tried to snatch her child from her. Stella tried to wake herself up again but she could not. Whenever she would awaken, she would immediately lapse right back into the dream again. Then the struggle would begin again. She fought to awaken. If only she would have the strength to sit up then the nightmare would cease.

The next morning her husband went over to see Anna and spoke to her about Stella's terrible night. Anna dropped everything and came over to see her daughter. She insisted that Stella have the baby baptized immediately. She poured wax over both the infant and Stella and said prayers over both of them. Both Stella and the infant seemed to improve after that.

Bill found himself a girlfriend. She was a lovely girl from Kitchener. Actually Bill had met her several times before through the CYO. They had danced and mingled but had not become serious. Anna, of course, was not very pleased. No girl was good enough for her sons, especially Bill. She wanted the best for him. Bill's girlfriend was a very religious person too and they made a lovely couple. They both loved the church and attended all the functions at the church. Everyone adored them and thought they made a great couple. On weekends Bill would bring his girlfriend down to Stella's house and she would stay there overnight in the extra bedroom. It was a good arrangement. This way Bill could see her and not have to bring her to his home to argue with Anna and embarrass his girlfriend.

Stella liked Bill's girlfriend and asked her to be Adele's Godmother at the christening. She agreed and arrangements were made to have the baby baptized. When Anna found out that Stella had not asked Anne to be the Godmother, she was furious. She insisted that Stella replace the Godmother immediately. Stella held her ground and would not back off for her mother. It was her child and she would do as she pleased with regards to who the child's Godmother would be. Anna refused to attend at the christening. Adele was christened and later Stella had prepared a wonderful meal for the Godparents. Everything was carried out in accordance with her plans and Stella was happy with the way things had turned out.

Stella would have to pack all the dirty diapers into the buggy with her baby and walk to her mother's place to wash them. She did not have a washing machine and either did her diapers at home by boiling them or would make the trip to Anna's place. With the mortgage payments, they found it a real hardship to purchase anything else, especially a washing machine.

Anna was busy again renovating the place. She hired a carpenter to come down and add a room to the kitchen side of her house. This brought the building even closer to the railway tracks. It was a large room but they did not install any heating ducts or electrical baseboard heaters. As a result it was very cold in the winter time. Anna had plans on moving into the room herself with Metro.

One day Anna suggested that Stella sell her house and move in with them. They had this extra room off the kitchen and it would be large enough for the crib as well as the bed. They could also share the kitchen facilities. Stella thought it was a good idea and they did sell their house within a few months after they purchased it. It was closer for her husband to go to work and was within walking distance so her husband was agreeable. Besides, they would no longer have to make mortgage payments on the house.

Anna immediately hired a carpenter again and he enclosed the living room in the front of the house. Anna converted it into a bedroom for herself and Metro. They moved the living room furniture into the large dining room and actually it looked quite nice.

Peter had also found a girlfriend. Her name was Helen. They fell in love and they were married that summer. They slept on the floor in the living room their first night. They moved in with her parents as Anna's place was too crowded.

Bill got engaged that summer. They set the date for their wedding on November 5th, 1949. They were going to get married in Kitchener as this was the wish of his bride-to-be.

Andrew came down for the big wedding. He had his hotel built and business was good he reported. The crowds were big and he stayed at the hotel and kept a watchful eye on everything at the hotel by living on the premises. He was still drinking and Anna had to accept him as he was.

Mary too arrived for the wedding with her children from Fork River. Her husband did not accompany her as he was busy with the farm and the animals. Mary stayed over at Michael's place and everyone was happy to see her.

The day of the wedding arrived and Bill's fiancé looked beautiful in her white gown. It was a fairly large wedding and everyone attended. It was the first time that the entire family was assembled together in years. Bill was very nervous but pleased.

The next day it was arranged that everyone attend at Michael's place to have the family portrait taken. It was the first time in years that the entire family had converged together and it would be a great time for the portrait taking. A photographer was hired to attend and everyone posed for the pictures. First the family gathered around Anna and Metro. There were twelve children. Six boys and six girls. Then the entire group with all their children had their picture taken. It was a very special occasion and Anna was very pleased. It showed by her expression that she was very proud.

Anna and Metro Kuzyk Family 1949

Chapter 44

Christmas Party 1949

In the meantime, Johnny decided to use this time to find himself a place to live. Anne occupied one of the bedrooms upstairs. Anna and Metro shared the converted front room downstairs. Stella and her husband slept in the newly built bedroom off the kitchen. Bill had discussed with Johnny about converting the one bedroom upstairs into a kitchen for him and his new wife. They would occupy the other bedroom upstairs.

Johnny had made arrangements with a carpenter to add stairs to the back of the house for entrance to the upper floor into the now converted kitchen. They had a door built into the kitchen. He fixed the kitchen up and had a stove and refrigerator installed for Bill. Johnny and Bill got along very well and would do anything for one another. By the time Bill and his wife got back from California, they had a self contained apartment all ready for them. Bill was very pleased. His wife got herself a job at a dry cleaning establishment and Bill drove her to work every day. Anne was still going to school. Anne and Bill's wife eventually became very good friends.

Suddenly one day, Bill was having trouble with his back. He went to see a doctor and was told that he had a slipped disk. A friend of his from the church told him to come and see him. He was a Chiropractor and told Bill that he could help him. Bill would go to see him. His friend would manipulate the area of soreness and Bill would go home feeling much better.

Christmas 1949 arrived and Michael reminded everyone that they had promised to gather at his place again for a reunion. Everyone attended at Michael's place except Johnny. Johnny always had other plans and did not go to these reunions. As usual, they brought their musical instruments along and everyone played and sang. Jessie and her husband were there as was Pauline and her husband. Bill and his new wife were there as well. They ate, drank, sang and played the guitar. Stella and her husband walked the few blocks with the baby carriage to Michael's place. Adele was 7-l/2 months old. They had no car to drive around in so they packed the baby into a buggy and walked the distance to Michael's house.

Bill's wife was starting to miss work a great deal. The family reached the conclusion that she too was pregnant and was expecting. She was having morning sickness and it became obvious to everyone. She eventually quit her job and stayed at home. She did not complain, but it was also apparent that she was not happy with the living accommodations. They only had the kitchen and bedroom to manoeuvre in and she was used to living in a larger place.

They discussed buying another house in the spring. Bill had a talk with Anna about it. He told Anna that she and Metro could continue to live in the house as long as they wished. He and his wife would buy a place of their own and they would even take Anne with them and support her schooling while she was with them. Anna would not have to worry about her. Anna hit the roof. She became infuriated with Bill and accused him of trying to take away her baby daughter. Not as long as she lived was she going to let this happen. She was uncontrollable. Bill backed off immediately and tried to reassure her that it was only an idea. Anne was nineteen years old and she was starting college that fall.

That May, Bill and his wife found a three bedroom home on the outskirts of Hamilton. It was a rural property and they fell in love with it. They had plans on moving into their new home within 60 days.

Bill Kuzyk and Stella Maga Wedding

Chapter 45

The Elopement

Sonia had met this man and she fell in love with him. They had secretly eloped and were married. Or so she thought. Approximately two weeks into the marriage, Sonia learned that he had previously married but their divorce had not been finalized . As a result their marriage was annulled. There would be a trial Sonia was told. She was very unhappy about it. She was frightened of attending before the Judge and testifying against the man she had loved. At the trial, Sonia had appeared before the Judge and testified to the facts as she knew them to be. The man had not told her that he had been previously married and talked her into eloping with him. Not even her family had been notified of the marriage. She also testified that she was now pregnant. The family stuck close to Sonia. Anna in particular rallied around her daughter and supported her in every respect. They were a loving family when it came to something which required their backing. Eventually, Sonia settled down and became her normal self. Anna kept a watchful eye on her just the same.

It was July and Bill and his wife were starting to pack their belongings ready for the move to their very own house. They were very happy and looking forward to their new place. Anna insisted that she would not stay in the old house. She would get her own place too. She did not need Bill's charity. He could sell the house because she was not going to stay there either.

When Bill and his wife moved out, Anna approached Johnny to buy a house. She had found this corner piece of property just around the block from where they were now and it had an upstairs apartment which was self contained. They could rent that apartment out and make mortgage payments on the house with the money they would be receiving from the rental. She had a few dollars saved up and would be willing to invest it in the house. She had seen the place. It was closer to the church too. Johnny listened to Anna and went to see the place himself. He decided that if Anna wanted to invest her portion of the money towards the purchase price, he would go along with it. So they purchased the corner house. Anna was very happy. She and Metro shared the one room on the main floor. Sonia and Anne shared one bedroom and Johnny had a bedroom to himself. They also shared a large bathroom off the small bedroom which Anna and Metro occupied.

There was a central room which was utilized as a large living room. A family room with a fireplace was situated just off Johnny's bedroom. A large kitchen was located off the large living room. There was also a small veranda by the entrance of the house and Metro enjoyed sitting out and saying his rosary. Johnny had placed a large sofa on the veranda for Metro and during the summer days, he would sometimes lie down on the sofa and fall asleep.

Anna was getting ambitious again. She talked Johnny into building a bedroom to the side of the house off the kitchen and making it into a self contained apartment. They had rented the upstairs apartment and were getting a fair amount for the rent. Johnny agreed to the extension and soon a carpenter arrived and commenced to build the one room off the kitchen. It was a long and narrow room but it was large enough to accommodate a bed and a small dresser. They installed a door to the narrow bedroom off the kitchen. A small bathroom with a shower was built into the kitchen area. Anna moved Metro into the narrow bedroom and he was content to be by himself and did not complain.

Anna had Sonia to look after. This pleased her. Sonia was starting to show and Anna catered to her every whim. Anne was preparing to enter college. Metro was receiving his old age security and this gave Anna even more money to manoeuvre with.

Bill and his wife moved into their own place and were happily settled down. They bought new furniture for the three bedroom home. Their friends from the church visited them often and life was wonderful for them.

One day shortly after Anna and her family had moved out, Stella and her husband discussed their situation at the house. This left them all alone in the big house. They agreed that they did not want to move anywhere at the present time and possibly they should ask Bill if they could rent the place. Stella thought that they should buy the house and pay Bill the money on a monthly basis. They could rent the upstairs apartment, which was now self contained, and this amount could be offset against the mortgage if they bought the place. It seemed like a good idea and they approached Bill and his wife about it. Bill and his wife agreed that they would sell the place to Stella and her husband for $5,000. It was such a reasonable amount and they agreed on a monthly payment to Bill in lieu of the mortgage. No interest charges were asked for. Bill was so thoughtful. So it was that Stella and her husband were now the owners of a house again.

They rented the apartment upstairs to a lovely Italian couple with a little boy. They in turn rented the small bedroom to an acquaintance of theirs and this helped them pay their rent to Stella and her husband. They all shared the bathroom upstairs. Anna and her family were just around the corner from Stella's place and they visited each other on a daily basis. It was a great arrangement and everyone was happy.

Peter Kuzyk and Helen Stayshyn Wedding

Chapter 46

Scary Intruder

Anna and Sonia started to play bingo together. They went to the hall under the church at first. Then they started to go to other places with bigger cash winnings. Anna could not read or write in any language, but she sure could play bingo. She progressed so quickly that she was playing as many as fifteen cards at once. She would win quite frequently.

Sonia eventually gave birth to a little girl. With Anna's help, she rented herself a big house not too far away. She leased it out to other people to help pay for the rent so that she in fact, was not paying any money for herself and lived rent free.

Two months later Stella gave birth to her second child. It was a boy and she named him Gary. He was born on October ll, 1950. Bill's wife also gave birth a couple of weeks later to a son. He was born on October 26, 1950 and they also named him Gary. They were not aware that Stella had named her son Gary as well.

Johnny went deer hunting one November day with a friend of his. On their way up north, Johnny lost control of the car he was driving and they hit a large rock cropping. Both he and his friend were thrown clear of the car and were taken to hospital in serious condition. Anna was crushed when she heard the news. Johnny was in a hospital up north and Anna could not visit him. Gradually both of them improved and were released from hospital. Anna was very thankful that they had not been injured permanently in some way and thanked God for saving her son again. He seemed to have a thing with vehicles and this frightened Anna.

Johnny renovated the basement downstairs, made two liveable rooms down there and rented them out too. He also built a small washroom which was shared by two of the men who rented the rooms. Anna was happy again, she was 62. She had a responsibility, it involved money and she was satisfied. She still played bingo with Sonia almost on a nightly basis. Metro was not feeling very well but he was not too sick to leave at home by himself, so Anna could get away whenever she wanted to.

Stella and her husband bought a new Pontiac. Her husband took their little girl with him to bring the car home. Stella was excited about the new car and cleaned up the house and did her laundry. She was anxious to get the clothes hung out on the line and then sit on the front porch to await her husband and their new car.

Baby Gary was just nine months old. He was sitting in his baby chair in the kitchen beside the door leading to the upstairs apartment. Stella was in the basement putting another load of clothes into the washing machine. She quickly ran upstairs and entered the living room. Through the open doorway into the kitchen she saw a man standing beside the back door in the kitchen. He was scruffy looking with bloodshot eyes and he had a dirty plaid shirt on. Stella became very frightened but did not want to show it. She immediately entered the kitchen to make sure her baby was not harmed. Gary was playing with his rattle and was making happy sounds. Stella asked the man angrily what he was doing in her house. He did not answer her but merely stared at her. He smelled of stale liquor and Stella became even more frightened. She told him he had better leave or she would call the man upstairs. He said why not call him then. Stella knew the people upstairs were not at home. She saw the lady leaving to go shopping fifteen minutes earlier. The husband had gone to work first thing that morning. Stella was desperate. She knew she could not take the time to grab her son out of his chair. She rushed passed the man and headed straight for the front door. Her screams brought the two men across the road who were mowing their lawns, quickly to her house. Meanwhile, the scruffy man in the plaid shirt slowly came out of the gate in the alley. He insisted he had done nothing to harm anyone and proceeded down the street away from the house.

Later one of the neighbours came over to see Stella and she advised that it was her brother-in-law who had caused her the stress. He had been playing poker all night and was drinking heavily. He had also heard that the Italian man renting the bedroom upstairs at Stella's house, had the same last name as he did and he wondered if they were related.

Stella's husband eventually arrived with their new Pontiac. After that Stella always made sure that the back door was locked as well as the front door. It had been a terrifying experience for her and left a mark on her for the rest of her life. She developed a thing about locking doors.

Anna received a letter from Andrew. He was now writing to a couple of ladies from overseas. He got their names and addresses from a magazine and the "lonely hearts club". They exchanged photographs and he had to make a choice as to what girl he wanted to send the fare to. Andrew was 36 years old.

Anna's girl's got together and presented her with a beautiful family ring. It was a token of their admiration and love for their wonderful mother.

Anna and Her Daughters

Chapter 47

Blushing Bride

Andrew went to the bank and arranged for a loan and now was sole owner of the Creighton hotel. He wrote that everything was fine now. He was making payments to the bank instead of his partners. Anna was relieved. She wrote that she would come and visit Andrew as soon as she possibly could.

Anne had entered college in Toronto. Anna was very proud of her young daughter. Anne had been dancing at the hall under the church and met a chap at the dance by the name of Tom Manzuk. They were writing to each other and he considered Anne to be his girlfriend. Anna knew his parents and they were very good people. Tom was their only son and Anna approved of the man.

Stella was expecting again. She obtained a job as a waitress in a local restaurant. Her husband worked steady days and she went to work evenings from 5 p.m. to 1 a.m. It worked out very well, as her husband could watch the children in the evening.

Bill's wife was expecting too. So was Peter's wife Helen. Bill's wife had another son. So did Peter's wife and Stella had another son Eddy, born March 18, 1952. Stella still continued to work at the restaurant and make some money.

One day Anna approached Pauline and asked her if she would like to go to Flin Flon to see Andrew. Pauline agreed and the two of them set out by train to visit Andrew. They stayed at the hotel with Andrew for the entire ten days. Pauline did some visiting of old friends she knew and renewed old acquaintances. It was a fun trip for her. Anna was happy to see Andrew and to know that he was doing fine with the business. They returned to Hamilton and Anna was feeling much better after their visit.

Anne quit college and came home to stay with Anna. She and Tom were engaged now and they were making plans for their wedding. They had set a date of August 29, 1953 as their wedding day. Anna was very thrilled with her daughter's wedding plans and made preparations with the women from the church to do the cooking and other matters to do with the wedding.

It was to be a big wedding. Anne purchased a beautiful white gown for herself. She also asked Stella to allow her daughter Adele to be the flower girl. This pleased Stella very much and she made her daughter a beautiful white tiered gown for the wedding. Anne took her mother shopping and they purchased a very trendy long dress suitable for a mother to wear at her daughter's wedding. Anna looked much younger than her 65 years. Everyone danced, ate and drank and had a wonderful time. Anne looked breathtaking in her wedding gown. She had long blonde hair and it was curled slightly into a page boy. Metro walked her down the isle and presented her to her husband-to-be. Anne looked extremely happy and Anna was joyous. Later Metro was not feeling too well and he was taken home early by one of the family members.

Anne and Tom were living at his parents home. Tom was going to start teaching school and they had no idea where they would be living. It depended on where he would get a job. They decided to stay with his parents until he found a position. They were very happy and Anna was pleased.

Anna and Sonia still played bingo every night. Anna had extra money from the renting of the house and Johnny allowed her to keep some of the money for groceries and maintenance of the place.

Sonia had some problems with one of her tenants. The tenant decided that he would approach the landlord and rent the house himself. He eventually spoke to the landlord and Sonia was given notice to vacate the premises. She had no place to go with a small child. She had a few dollars saved up and decided she would use it as a down payment on a house. She bought a place on Burlington Street. It was not a very nice area but it was affordable. She rented out a portion of the place and this she used to offset the mortgage payments on the house.

Andrew wrote that he was still corresponding with a few ladies through the "lonely hearts club" but nothing had developed out of the correspondence. His business at the hotel was good and he was paying off the loan to the bank. Everything else was back to normal and he was quite content.

Bill and his wife bought a television set. They now had three children. Everyone was thrilled about the television. Stella and her husband came over to watch it and decided that they should get one too. It was awesome. Movies at home! Stella and her husband did purchase a television set of their own a couple of weeks later.

Anne was expecting a baby that June. She, like Stella, wanted to be close to Anna at such a special time. Anne and Tom moved in with Anna. The apartment on the main floor was not rented so Anna shared the kitchen with Anne and Tom and they slept in the addition off the kitchen.

Anne was expecting any day now and Anna kept a close watch on her. Tom was still at University and would be finishing his course that year. He had been offered a teaching job in Niagara Falls and they were planning on moving there after the summer holidays.

Stella was expecting her fourth child in October. She was very unhappy. Her husband took his holidays during the tobacco farms season and every summer he would go away to the farm and leave Stella alone with the children. She had to take public transportation everywhere she went with the three small children. She could not work during her pregnancy and had no money of her own to speak of.

Anne had a son born on June 27, 1954. She was very happy with the little boy and named him Tommy after his father. The baby cried a lot. Between Anne and her mother they would pace the floor with the child. Anne was exhausted. She was breast feeding the infant. Anna tried to tell her that the child was hungry and needed some solid food. Anne had been to the doctor's and he advised her that she should not give the infant any solid food for six weeks. Anne stuck to the Doctor's orders. No one got any sleep during the first three weeks. The baby would awaken every hour and scream continuously.

One night Anna told her daughter and her husband to go to a movie and get some rest. Going away for the evening would be good for them Anna advised. So off they went to the movies. As soon as they had gone, Anna left the infant with Metro and came over to see Stella. She told Stella that she needed some help. Little Tommy cried because he was hungry. She told Stella that Anne did not have sufficient milk to breast feed the infant. The child needed some solid food. Would Stella please bring some pabulum and her baby's formula and feed Anne's baby? Stella was terrified to go against the wishes of Anne and her doctor. She refused to interfere. Anna begged Stella and stated that she would not tell a soul about it. Especially not Anne.

Stella took a teaspoon of pabulum she had for her baby and a bottle of formula and went over with Anna to her place. She heated up the formula and mixed it with the teaspoon of pabulum and fed the infant. He had been screaming before she fed him. He ate the teaspoon of pabulum with gusto. As soon as he had eaten the pabulum, Stella gave him a bottle of formula. The child fell asleep immediately and for the first time since he was brought home, the infant slept right through the night. Anne and Tom and the entire house had a good night's sleep that night.

Stella was fearful of being found out. She had not wanted to get involved in the situation. However, she was involved and she hoped and prayed that everything would go well with the baby. The very next day Anna convinced Anne that she had to get a formula for her baby because, like herself, Anne did not have sufficient milk to satisfy her infant. He was hungry and that is why he cried. Anne did go to see her doctor again and the infant was put on the same formula as Stella's baby. Stella was relieved. She never told anyone about the feeding incident and kept the secret to herself.

Anne and her husband stayed at Anna's place for the entire summer holidays. Tom got a job working for the summer and they made plans to move to Niagara Falls before school started. They had gone to Niagara Falls and purchased a house there. The closing date was the end of August and gave them plenty of time to make the move before school started.

After Anne and Tom moved out Anna rented their bedroom, kitchen and bathroom as an apartment. It was self contained and Anna shared her bedroom with Metro.

Stella and her husband put their house up for sale. They had purchased a two acre plot of land in Waterdown and were planning on building a new home under the Veteran's Land Act. They had to move out of their house when it was sold. Their new home was not ready yet so they had to rent an apartment. They rented an upstairs apartment. Stella was expecting in October and was heavy with child.

Tom Manzuk and Anne Kuzyk Wedding

Chapter 48

Babies, Babies Everywhere

Mary's oldest son Pete came to Hamilton in August, 1954. Johnny immediately rallied around and got his nephew a job working as a bell hop at the hotel. Pete soon met a wonderful gal and they returned to Fork River to get married there. He was not quite twenty years old when they got married. They eventually returned to Hamilton and settled down to raise a family.

Stella gave birth to another son on October 26, 1954. They named him James Peter. He was a healthy baby and Stella was very happy with her new son. She was anxious to move into their new home the following summer.

Eventually Stella had a run-in with the landlady and she and her family moved out to an apartment across the road from the hospital on John Street where they stayed until their new house in Waterdown would be ready for occupancy. There was still a lot to be done in the interior of the house. They had plans on moving into it by the time their lease expired whether it was ready or not. If need be, they could always move into the basement if the house upstairs was not ready.

One day Johnny decided that he needed a change. He had some money saved up and wanted to start a business venture. He quit his job at the hotel, packed his suitcase and flew to Cuba. He met an American chap there. He was a Polish fellow with a long name so Johnny called him "Ski" for short. Together they purchased a piece of property and started a driving range on the Isle of Pines. Johnny also opened up a dry cleaning and laundry business for himself in Havana. He had hired someone to operate it while he was involved in the driving range.

Both businesses were doing great and eventually Johnny built himself a beautiful home on the Isle of Pines with a marble driveway. He would come home to visit now and again and do his banking in Hamilton with the money he received from the apartments which Anna rented out.

While he was away, Anna would collect the rent from the apartments for Johnny. They now had the apartment upstairs and the one on the main floor she was renting. In Johnny's absence, Anna had built on to Johnny's bedroom and added a sink and stove to his room and did all her cooking out of his bedroom. She kept the refrigerator in her bedroom. It was crowded, but Anna was used to that.

One day the people in the apartment on the first floor moved out. Johnny insisted that Anna do her cooking in the other kitchen. He did not like the idea of having someone in his room doing the cooking and washing the dishes. Anna insisted that he was away a great deal and did not use the room much anyway. Johnny won the argument and so it was that they rented out the back bedroom to a man from the church. He was in his late fifties and was a bachelor. He shared the kitchen with Anna and they became quite friendly. Metro was very jealous of the man and he and Anna argued about him constantly.

A few months later Anna's boarder the bachelor, got involved with a woman from the church. He brought her to Anna's place and made her a cup of tea. They sat together in his bedroom off the kitchen. He closed the door to his room for some privacy. They could be heard talking and laughing. Anna became very upset. She was not going to tolerate any of that sort of behaviour in her house. The man had no right to bring any woman to her place and carry on the way they did. The man was stunned. Johnny, who was visiting at the time from Cuba, intervened and told Anna that it was none of her business. It was such a mess that the man decided the best thing to do was to move out which he did. Anna still considered that what she did was the right thing. She did not want her house to be considered a red light district she said. Anna did not rent out the room again. Instead she talked Johnny into closing off the area again with the kitchen and the bathroom and renting it out as an apartment. This they did and Anna was back cooking on Johnny's stove in his bedroom again.

Anne and her husband had moved to Niagara Falls and he was teaching in a school there. They were very happy and Anna was very pleased with them. Anne had a natural talent. She started to paint with oils and was very good at it. Anna's sister Dora had been down for a visit and had admired Anne's work. Later she wrote and asked if Anne could do some painting for her church in Swift Current. Anne agreed and did the fourteen stations of the cross for a little church on the prairies. It was quite a project and Anna again was very proud of her daughter and her wonderful talents.

Peter and his wife Helen now had two children and she was on the way with her third. Peter had built his own home in Stoney Creek and things appeared to be going well with them. He was working at an automobile company and was involved with body and fender work.

Fred was overjoyed. His wife was finally expecting a baby and she had carried over the two month period. Her doctor watched her closely. She was still on the special medication and Fred bragged to everyone about the coming baby. Anna warned him not to be too enthusiastic in case his wife should have another miscarriage. Fred catered to his wife's every need and forbade her to do any work that might cause her to miscarry. Fred's wife finally gave birth to a son. Labour was induced at seven months as the doctor was concerned about her carrying beyond that time. The child was born on January 24, 1956. They named him Fred after his father.

Stella and her family finally moved into their new home in Waterdown. It was completed to their satisfaction. She was expecting her fifth child the following October. Stella gave birth to a little girl on October 29th, 1956. She called her Arlene. Anna was brought over to see the new baby Arlene. She said how beautiful the baby was and placed a silver dollar in Arlene's tiny hand. Stella wondered at the rate she was going, if she would surpass her mother in the number of children she would eventually have. Her mother did not start until she was 26 years old. Stella was only nineteen when she had her first child.

Bill's wife was also due with her fifth child too. Anne was pregnant too with her second baby. It seemed like everyone in the family was expecting at the same time. All the women in Anna's family were pregnant. Anna was very pleased.

Stella and William Duschl Family

Chapter 49

Death of the Patriarch

Metro was not feeling very well. He did not complain very often but everyone could tell he was sick. Anna still played bingo and was away almost nightly.

Anna received a letter from Andrew. He finally found the girl of his dreams. She was a German girl and he would be bringing her to Flin Flon very shortly. She was divorced from her husband and had a little boy by him. The lad was six years old. She was dark and very pretty according to his picture of her. They had exchanged photographs and it was agreed that she would marry him as soon as she arrived in Canada from Germany. She was well educated and could read and write as well as speak the English language.

One day Metro became seriously ill. He could not control his bladder. He complained of chest pains and the family thought he was having a heart attack. He was transported to the Henderson General hospital. The family was very unhappy about his treatment there. Stella thought the nurses were very mean to her father. They would make him use the treadmill even though he begged to stop. There was a heavy set nurse who yelled at him and told him to keep it up. Stella could not stand to watch it and she left the room.

Later when Stella visited her father, he was lying in bed and complained about a terrible pain in his groin. He was attached with a bag to drain his bladder and something was not right. Stella had gone to the nurse's station to complain about the pain he was feeling. She waited for an hour and still no one came to ease his pain. Finally she had to leave as her husband was waiting in the car in the parking lot with the children and she could not stay with Metro any longer. A month later, Metro was released from hospital and returned home. Anna had to tend to his every need. He was still attached to the bag and a Victorian nurse came down a couple of times a week to check on him. For a long time Metro remained in bed. He could get up and go to the bathroom with some assistance even with his bag still attached. Anna could go and play bingo and leave him alone. She was still tied down to the house a lot.

Anna was beginning to play bingo day and night and it was getting to be a little too much. She would go and play bingo in the afternoon for three hours. Then she would also go out at night. Johnny reprimanded Anna for playing so much bingo when he was home from Cuba. Anna felt a need to get away. It was like when her children were small. She just had to get away from Metro too for a while.

Johnny came down for a visit from Cuba again. He was very concerned about the situation developing in that country. Fidel Castro was creating a lot of problems. His friend Ski was talking about leaving Cuba and returning to the United States. There was talk about Americans in Cuba fearing for their lives. The Canadians were not as fearful, but Johnny was still concerned about the business aspect of it as well as his own safety.

Stella came down to see her father one afternoon. She knocked on the door and no one answered, so she came in anyway. Something was not right. There was a terrible odour about the house. She went into the bedroom where Metro slept and the stench was overwhelming. Her father had tried to get up to go to the bathroom and could not make it in time. He had soiled himself, the floor and the bed. He was now lying in it. He was very happy to see Stella. She cried when she saw him. He looked so pathetic. Stella found a clean sheet and then she scrubbed Metro clean and changed the bedding with him in the bed. It was difficult, but she managed. She then cleaned up the floor and waited for Anna to come home. Metro advised that Anna had gone to play bingo.

Stella was very upset with Anna. When Anna returned home, Stella lit into her and admonished Anna. Anna just sat with her head bowed and said nothing. It was so unusual for her to have nothing to say. Later Stella was very sorry for talking to her mother that way. After all Anna was seventy one years old and she needed a break from Metro and all the attention he required from her. Bingo was her only outlet. Bingo was the only thing she got any enjoyment from and she certainly deserved it. Stella was ashamed and later apologized to her mother and asked for her forgiveness for the remarks she had made.

Johnny wrote home and said that his friend Ski had suddenly fled Cuba with his life. He left everything he had behind him and was lucky to escape Castro and his wrath. Johnny was getting threatening telephone calls and his life was in danger as well. He said that he had a few things he wanted to do first and then he too would be leaving the country as soon as possible. They would not even let them take any American money with them. Johnny said that he would bury some of it and maybe one day return to retrieve it. Suddenly Johnny was home. He too had fled the country with his life. Everything he had worked so hard for was gone. He considered himself lucky to be alive. He was glad to be home in Canada. The year was 1959.

Sonia had found herself a wonderful man. His name was Dan Haradyn. He was from the church and Anna was ecstatic. They were deeply in love with one another and there was talk of marriage. They had not set a date as yet but Sonia was engaged.

Metro was suddenly rushed back into hospital again. This time he was taken to the Hamilton General. He was very ill. The doctors did not know what was wrong with him. One day as Sonia was visiting him he gave out a gasp, his eyes closed and he passed away. Sonia was devastated and called the nurses. They checked his heart and pulse and confirmed that Metro was gone. He died on September 7, 1959. He was in his seventy-third year. The entire family was very upset with the news, even though it had been expected. The hospital requested that an autopsy be performed to determine the cause of death. The family agreed and an autopsy was done on Metro. They could not establish the cause of death, merely that Metro had boil-like sores throughout his lungs and this was possibly the reason for his illness.

Andrew and his new wife flew in from Flin Flon to be at the funeral. His wife was shorter than Andrew. She was very petite and pretty. She had long black hair and they made a very handsome couple. Andrew proudly introduced her to the family as "his" wife. She could speak English fluently and appeared to be a very nice lady.

Mary also came from Fork River to be at her father's funeral. She came alone and stayed at her son's place.

Sonia and Dan decided to postpone their wedding plans for an entire year in honour of the passing of Metro. It was a big funeral and he was buried in the Holy Sepulchre Cemetery just outside of Hamilton.

Anna was blamed for a lot of things during Metro's lifetime. However, it was Anna who had saved him, with God's help of course, those many years ago when even the doctor had given him only six months to live. She bore him many children and looked after him when he was ailing. He also had a good and long life and Anna had no regrets.

Metro Kuzyk

Chapter 50

Buffalo Bingo

Michael and his wife Jean became separated. Their oldest daughter was working. Their son joined the army and was now stationed in Egypt with the peace keeping mission.

Sonia made plans for a wedding in the late summer of 1960. She and Dan set a date as August 20th for their wedding day. Anna was very pleased for her daughter. Her husband to be was a Catholic and he was Ukrainian. He was a God fearing man and this made Anna extremely happy.

It was a big wedding. All of his friends and family attended as did Sonia's family and friends. Sonia looked absolutely beautiful in her gown. It was a very unusual type of gown. It started just below the knees in the front and slowly tapered off into a small train in the back. They made a lovely couple and were very much in love. Sonia's small daughter was her flower girl and she looked as beautiful as her mother. As usual, Anna sang as she presented her money in the plate on the table in front of the bride and groom.

Johnny was anxious to get into some sort of business for himself. He was still communicating with his friend in the United States. Ski came down to see Johnny and they discussed a business venture. It was decided that they should purchase a farm and convert a portion of it into a driving range. They had so much success with the driving range in Cuba that they thought they should try it in Canada.

They located a farm on the waterfront in Port Dover. It had a big farm house on the property with a barn and a large shed. They immediately brought Bill into the transaction and the three of them purchased the property. Ski would eventually sell out his share and Johnny and Bill would become sole owners. There were other cottages in the area on the water and the deed stipulated that they had to supply the cottagers with water for a period of twenty years. Johnny, Bill and Ski had agreed and so they purchased the farm.

It was a wonderful change for Bill and his family. They now had five children and on week ends the family would come down to the farm house and spend a fantastic two days on the water. The children especially enjoyed the farm. They spent most of the time in the water. His wife was happy to have a place to spend their week ends at. They fixed the old house up and there were plenty of rooms to accommodate everyone.

Anna continued to play bingo. Now that Metro was gone, she had more time to herself. A group of ladies who enjoyed playing bingo as much as Anna did, decided to charter a bus. On Sundays there was no bingo in Hamilton, so they rode to the United States on the chartered bus on Sunday and played bingo in Buffalo. The bus would then bring them back to Hamilton.

Andrew wrote home to say that he and his new wife were expecting a baby. He was extremely happy to make the announcement. Business was good and they were now living in his house.

Johnny decided on another business venture. The farm was great and Ski lived there to run the driving range. Johnny obtained a concession in the Hamilton bowling alley. It was a small restaurant with a kitchen in the back. It had stools to sit on at the counter. The people in the bowling alley would cater to the restaurant and Johnny was doing well. He hired himself a woman to do the cooking and had several young girls serving the food and drinks to the bowlers. He did a thriving business and was quite pleased about the turn of events.

Sonia and Dan were expecting their first child. They were both ecstatic. He was working in a jewellery store with his older brother who owned it. They purchased a new house in the east end of the city. Sonia as well as Anne, was very talented in an artistic way. She also took up oil painting. She painted a big mural on the wall in their living room. Sonia was as good as Anne was in painting pictures and her husband Dan was very proud of her.

Anna received another letter from Andrew. He and his wife had a little girl. They were not getting along very well and eventually divorced. Anna was worried about Andrew.

Dan Haradyn and Sonia Kuzyk Wedding

Chapter 51

Day of Sorrow

Stella and her husband separated and eventually divorced. Stella moved in with Anna and Anna was overjoyed to see her daughter back home. She arranged for Stella to sleep in the large dining room and Stella managed to move her twin bedroom set in the area as well.

Johnny again rallied around and told Stella she could have a job as the head cook at his bowling alley restaurant. He and his present cook were not getting along. She wanted their relationship to progress to boyfriend and girlfriend and Johnny refused to have anything to do with it. So he politely told her to move on and Stella started to work for Johnny.

Sonia and her husband Dan had a girl. A year later, they had a little boy. It was a perfect family and they appeared to be very happy. They had sold their new house at the east end of the city and purchased a big house just off Gage Avenue. They renovated it and rented out a portion of the place. This helped them to offset the mortgage payments on the house.

Anna still played bingo and would go out nightly. Johnny would scold her about it. Stella would intervene and tell Johnny to let her be. She was going on eighty years soon and deserved to enjoy herself a little bit after all she had been through.

Anna was very concerned about Peter. He had sold his house in Stoney Creek and purchased some property up north in Parry Sound. The property he purchased was out in the sticks, Anna said. Her heart ached for him and his family. She had talked Johnny into driving her over to see Peter and his family one week end and while she was there, a raven had smashed its way through the big picture window and landed on the living room floor. This was definitely a bad omen, Anna insisted and she tried to talk Peter into selling the place and getting out of there. Peter just grinned at his mother and said nothing.

Bill and his wife had decided that they would sell their old place on the outskirts of Hamilton. His wife had her eye on a beautiful new home in a subdivision going up on the Hamilton mountain. They eventually sold their house and purchased the new one. His wife was very happy and Bill worked hard to get the landscaping in. There was still some work to be completed in the basement but it was a beautiful home and they were very proud of it.

Two of Anna's children, Bill and Stella, each had five children, 3 boys and 2 girls and they only lived a few miles from each other. Both named their oldest boys Gary and they were born only two weeks apart. It must have been very confusing to Anna and the rest with both sets of parents named Bill and Stella.

Anna became very jealous one day. Stella had cooked a meal on her day off, including some delicious apple pie for them for dinner. Anna accused Stella of trying to show her up. She had been doing all the cooking for Johnny and now Stella shows up and suddenly she can cook better than Anna. Stella was heartsick. She was just trying to help she insisted. Stella could see that things were not going to work out for her at Johnny's place. One day she spoke to him about leaving and moving to Toronto. Johnny was very upset but he agreed to it. So Stella packed her suitcase and went to Toronto to get a job there. She had left her furniture at Johnny's place until she could find herself an apartment to rent.

Johnny and Bill were digging a well on the beach section of the farm in Port Dover. It was during the week and Bill and Johnny were busy working on the beach. Bill was operating the tractor and hauling some wood to build the framing for the well. Bill had been driving the tractor and somehow the traction of the wheels in the sand started to throw up the sand into the air and the tractor flipped over. The cast iron steering wheel landed on Bill's left thigh and the steering wheel broke in half. Bill was pinned under the tractor by the cast iron wheel. He lay under the wheel in terrible agony and screamed for help. Johnny managed to lift the tractor up and Bill rolled over from under the wheel. He could not move too much and lay there moaning in pain.

They immediately called the ambulance and drove Bill to the hospital in Hamilton. The doctors examined Bill and gave him some medication to take for the clotting of the blood. His leg was swollen so much it did not look like a leg. It was purple in colour from his knee to the top of his thigh. The decision of the doctors was not to keep Bill in the hospital for further observation. They released him and Bill went home to his family. That night the entire family gathered at Bill's new place and visited with him all evening. Anna was gravely concerned and thanked God that it was not any other part of his body that had been crushed.

The following morning, Bill's wife had gone out to do some shopping. Her son came home during the morning hours from school. He had an appointment to see his dentist and his mother was to drive him to the dentist's office. He entered the house and to his horror, he found his father laying on the floor. His father's hand was reaching into his shirt pocket where his pills were. Bill was very still and his son immediately started mouth to mouth resuscitation on his father. At that moment his wife came home and called the ambulance.

Bill was pronounced dead on arrival at hospital. They performed an autopsy on him and it was determined that a blood clot had rushed to his heart killing him instantly. The doctor suggested that it was better it went to his heart rather than to his brain. If it had gone to his brain, he may have turned out to be a vegetable for the rest of his life the doctor stated. It was Wednesday, May ll, 1966. Bill was 42 years of age.

Anna's heart was broken again. She was seventy eight years old and had buried another son named Bill. He had left five children behind and a wonderful wife he loved dearly. It was such a tragedy.

The family mourned him deeply. If anyone in the family had to eulogize Bill they would probably say that he was a very special type of person. They would also say that he was a caring brother, a loving father and a faithful husband. If a stranger shook his hand and said it was a pleasure to meet him, that stranger found himself meaning every word of it sincerely. That was the impression he left behind him with everyone he had ever met.

Bill Kuzyk

Chapter 52

Still Accident Prone

It was a big funeral. There were over 200 cars in the funeral procession. Everyone had loved Bill and came to pay their last respects to a wonderful man. His wife needed company during the first week of his burial. The entire family took turns sleeping at her place so that she would not be left alone. She prayed a great deal and this was helpful to her in many ways.

Shortly after Bill was buried, his wife put the new house up for sale. She could not afford to make the mortgage payments on the house. The new place sold very quickly. She purchased a big old house in the centre of the city and she and her family moved into the old house. She immediately began to look for a job and she soon obtained one. It kept her busy and she had her children to console her. Bill's wife was strong and would survive the loss.

Johnny immediately approached Bill's wife to sell Bill's share of the waterfront home in Port Dover. Bill's wife would miss the week end trips there with her children. At first there appeared to be a problem with Johnny buying her out. Eventually, she determined it was for the best and sold Bill's share to Johnny. Johnny was now the sole owner of the farm and he spent a great deal of time there himself. He would invite the family down for barbecues. He would fix the place up and keep improving it all the while running the restaurant at the bowling alley.

Anne and Tom had long since moved to Grimsby where her husband was teaching school. They bought a lot in Grimsby and decided that Grimsby was the place they would stay. Tom was teaching and taking a course in professorship. They wanted to build their own house on the lot and were looking forward to it.

Stella met a man named Lyle Noble. They became engaged and were married on December 17, 1968. Stella had not told anyone, neither did Lyle and they were secretly married at the old City Hall. Stella became Mrs. Lyle Noble and she moved into his apartment on Avenue Road. When Stella brought Lyle over to see her family, they were all very surprised and they liked Lyle very much. Anna was especially pleased to see Stella happy for a change. Lyle was quiet and gentle and very well mannered. He was a gentleman and everyone knew it. He was also a chartered accountant.

Johnny was dating a young lady he called "Teddy". She was a very pretty girl with long black hair. She was very small. Johnny seemed to like his woman to be petite. Anna had met Teddy and she, surprisingly enough, liked the girl very much and she told Johnny so.

Johnny was having trouble at the restaurant. It had been broken into several times and Johnny was starting to spend the nights at the restaurant. He was becoming a nervous wreck. Anna worried about him and warned him that some thugs could break in and kill him. Johnny moved to the farm in Port Dover and spent a great deal of his time fixing up the place. He would commute back and forth to Hamilton. Sometimes he would bring his girlfriend Teddy to the farm. She was very much in love with Johnny and professed her undying love for him constantly.

One day in January, 1969, as Johnny was driving the car with Teddy, he somehow lost control of the vehicle and had a terrible accident. He appeared not to be hurt too much, but Teddy was badly injured. She was in very serious condition. They were both driven by ambulance to the hospital where they advised Johnny that Teddy had a fifty percent chance of survival. Anna was devastated again. Her son was always involved in car accidents. Every time he entered a car, she feared for his life. She was driven to the hospital to see Johnny and his Teddy. As

Johnny improved, Teddy was still in serious condition. She looked so pathetic and tiny in the bed. Johnny became despondent. He would visit with Teddy and beg her to get better. In desperation, he promised her that he would marry her if only she got well. Gradually, Teddy improved. Johnny was soon released from hospital and was visiting Teddy on a regular basis.

Johnny would pick Anna up at the house now and again. He would take her down to the farm, give her a room and Teddy spent many hours looking after Anna. Anna would like to be catered to and she certainly liked Teddy.

Lyle Noble and Stella Kuzyk Duschl Wedding

Chapter 53

Hanky Panky

One day Johnny came to Hamilton by himself. He had to tend to some business and walked in on Anna unexpectedly. She was sitting on her bed with a gentleman who had his arms around her and they were kissing. When Anna spotted Johnny, her face turned many shades of red. Johnny quickly walked out of the room and was embarrassed by what he had seen. Anna was 82 years old and still going strong. She apparently had met the man at the church. They had become good friends. He bought Anna a beautiful dress and she proudly displayed it to her children. She said that they were very serious about one another. Like Anna, he too had children and they objected to the relationship very strenuously. Eventually the man stopped coming around and Anna was very disappointed. She had liked the man very much and enjoyed his company. Now she was alone again.

She did not go to many bingos any more. Her eyes were bothering her and she thought that she had cataracts in her eyes. She would rub them and her eyes would get red and swollen. Pauline took her to see an eye specialist and sure enough, she had cataracts and the doctor made arrangements to have her operated on. Anna was frightened but Pauline reassured her that there was nothing to be afraid of. Anna kept postponing the operation and insisted that she did not need it.

Anna still collected the rent for Johnny and looked after the old house for him. Occasionally, Johnny would bring Anna down to his place to give her a change of pace and she enjoyed being on the farm with Johnny and Teddy to cater to her every need. She felt very important. On April 2, 1972, Johnny and Teddy were married. Anna was happy. At long last her son was finally married. Johnny was 51 years old.

Anna had her cataracts removed when she was 84 years of age. She claimed that she could see a little bit better. There was not too much of an improvement though. The operation had been a success. Anna refused to wear eye glasses and therefore, without the glasses she could not see very well.

The following Christmas, Anna decided that she would make some moonshine again. She purchased some overripe peaches and let them ferment. She made a coke bottle full for each of her children. It was a Christmas present to the men in the family she said. It was very potent. Lyle could hardly drink the stuff it was that strong. Anna had not lost her touch. She always kept a small bottle of peach brandy beside her bed for medicinal purposes. The children were very much surprised as Anna never drank when she was younger. This was quite a revelation.

One day Anna got very ill. The children became very concerned about her. Anna had never had the time to be sick when she was younger. Her children were her source of inspiration. If she became ill, who would look after her children? This was the first time they realized that she was truly ailing.

Anne took her mother to see a specialist. He examined her and said that she had gall stones. It was a relatively normal operation, however, because of Anna's age, complications could set in. Anna refused to go to the hospital. She said that if she went, she would not return, just like Metro. The pain was unbearable and she finally conceded and was admitted into the hospital for surgery. The operation was a success and after two weeks, Anna was released and returned home. She was feeling much better but she was still very weak and exhausted. She was 85 years old.

Johnny took Anna home to the farm to recuperate. Teddy was very good with Anna and looked after her and prepared her meals for her.

Anna was very content to stay there with Johnny and his wife. Johnny was tiring of running back and forth from Hamilton to the farm. One day he discussed with Anna the idea of selling the house in Hamilton. Where would she live, Anna inquired? Johnny suggested that she get herself a small apartment close to the church. She would not need to worry herself about collecting the rent money. She was getting her pension now for quite some time and it would take care of the rental for the apartment.

So it was that Johnny finally sold the old house. It sold very quickly. Anna eventually found herself a small room across the road from the house. Johnny sold the furnishings with the house except for one item. Stella had always wanted the old oak piece of Anna's that she had used as her altar. Stella and Lyle picked it up one day before the closing date of the house and took it to their place. They had purchased a beautiful lot on a ravine and had their new house built on the lot. It was overlooking Lake Ontario and had a fantastic view of the area.

Anna had a telephone installed in her room and was quite content with her situation. She would call the girls every day and let them know how she was doing. She had an account with a small grocery store on Barton Street. It was called "Kustra's". She would run the bill up and pay it on a monthly basis. Things were working out pretty well for her. Her church was close by and so were all her friends.

Fred and Mary had two houses on Main Street, which they sold and purchased a big new house in Burlington. Fred was still very proud of his son and they took him everywhere with them. He was now sixteen years old and was attending high school. Fred bought him a guitar and he learned to play it very well. Fred said he was just like the rest of the Kuzyk family. They were all very talented. His son was also doing some modelling in Toronto and his parents were very pleased. He was a handsome young man and they could see many good things happening for him.

One day Anna befriended a man in the room upstairs. He had a separate entrance to his place from the back of the house. Anna would buy him his groceries sometimes and generally look after him. On this day, she had purchased something for him and knocked on his door to give it to him. There was no answer so she walked into the room. The man was lying in his cot and did not appear to have heard her. Anna walked over to him and shook him to wake him up. To her horror she realized that he was ice cold and stiff as a board. She gasped and quickly rushed outside and to her room. She called Pauline and told her that the man was dead. Pauline called the police who came down to investigate. Sure enough, the man had been dead for some time and rigor mortis had set in. It was a very frightening experience for Anna. Shortly after that she decided she would find another place to live.

Johnny and Teddy Kuzyk

Chapter 54

Shocking Secret Revealed

Anna had moved a couple of times since finding the old man dead. She moved in with a lady who had several small dogs. Anna was very unhappy there because she claimed the dogs smelled and yapped constantly. Eventually she moved again to an apartment on a corner of the street in the basement. It was a cold and damp place and the children worried about her health.

She still attended the church and did her own cooking. Michael lived close by and would drop in on her almost daily for a visit.

She had some peach brandy and Michael would have his daily libation. Anna finally located an apartment with the help of the children in the same building only it was on the second floor. It was a two room place. One room she used as a kitchen, being the smaller of the two rooms, and one room she used as her bedroom, living room. She was very happy there and would purchase her candles from the church. She would pray and burn them constantly.

Anna's sister Dora had arrived for a visit from Saskatchewan. Since Anna was living in a small apartment and could not accommodate Dora, the children took turns in having both of them down for a few days. Dora was going to be staying for a month and intended to spend some time with her own daughter, who lived in Mississauga, for a week before returning home.

It was the end of May and Anna had just celebrated her 87th birthday. Johnny decided that it might be a good way for everyone to meet with Dora, by throwing a birthday party for Anna at his place in Port Dover. Most of Anna's children were there with their offspring and a wonderful time was had by all. They brought their own drinks, they danced and ate and later Anna opened her birthday presents and was very aloof about the whole affair.

Stella and Lyle had a beautiful home on the outskirts of Toronto. It was situated on a ravine lot with Lake Ontario in the background. They also had an in-ground swimming pool and this was why Anna wanted to come, so she could show off to Dora. There was a great deal of rivalry between the two of them. Every evening they would wait outside for Stella's husband Lyle to arrive from work and would rush to kiss him. Stella cooked chicken soup for them and prepared lunches and they were having a good time. Every afternoon they would have a nap. They each had a room of their own and it was a perfect arrangement.

One afternoon when Lyle arrived home, he took out the tape recorder and Anna and Dora sang songs together. Songs they used to sing in the old country on stage. Lyle taped it and played it back to them. They giggled with delight when they heard themselves singing. Stella thought that things were going pretty well. They stayed at Stella's place for almost two weeks. Anna had brought along some herbs and spices and decided that Stella needed some healing. She placed the concoction in a foil plate on the floor and had Stella stand over it while the spices burned. She then had Dora hold a pan of cold water over Stella's head. Then she poured the hot wax into the pan while she prayed. Stella did not believe in any of the things Anna was doing, but if it made her mother happy, so be it. She was glad that Lyle was not home to see this. Dora too made faces behind Anna's back. Stella went along with it.

One afternoon when they were having their nap, Stella was surprised to see Dora come down the stairs. Her aunt said she couldn't sleep and wanted Stella to come outside on the patio. She had something she said to tell her. She sounded so mysterious and Stella was curious. Stella prepared cool drinks for them and they went out on the patio. Anna was still asleep. Dora related the following. In the old country when Anna was in her late teens, she met this extremely handsome young soldier. They fell in love and the soldier promised Anna he would marry her when he came back from the war. He got Anna pregnant. When her father found out, he threatened Anna with her life.

Then the devastation began. When Anna started to show, she was the talk of the village. The boys jeered at her. The girls pointed fingers at her and whispered behind her back. Anna felt so ashamed and humiliated. She was all alone. She wanted to run away and hide only there was no place to go or hide. In the old country a girl was considered used goods if she got pregnant before marriage. This is how they made Anna feel. She felt wretched and miserable. She was also very strong and somehow managed to survive the pregnancy. Anna had a little girl.

Stella asked Dora what happened to the little girl. Dora said that one day when Anna went to the orchard to work, she left the baby girl with her father who was to look after the infant. Upon her return from the orchard, she found the little one had passed away. No one knew what happened. Anna had been overcome with grief. Stella thought that perhaps it was a crib death.

Stella felt like asking her aunt Dora why she was telling her all this about her mother, but she held her tongue. She suspected that Dora got a great deal of pleasure telling Anna's secret to her children. All these many years Anna had kept a secret about herself from her children. She was so strict with all her girls about romances and yet here she made the very mistake she wanted to keep her girls from making. Later Stella found out that Dora had also told the others the same story. Why, the children could not figure it out, but they suspected that Dora was getting even with Anna about something.

When Anna woke up and came downstairs later that afternoon, she looked surprised and somehow Stella knew that her mother felt she had been discussed. There was an awkward silence and Stella knew that Anna had a feeling that something was not right. Stella could not look

Dora in the eye after this discussion and somehow her aunt realized this and decided it was time to leave for her daughter's place.

Later Fred asked Anna about the first child she had and told her that Dora had related the details to all the children. He also tried to convince her that knowing about Anna's firstborn, did not change the way her children felt about her. Anna was overwhelmed with shame. She vowed never to speak to Dora again and she never did. Dora left for Saskatchewan and subsequently Anna heard that Dora's children had placed their mother in a nursing home where she later passed away.

Anna and Sister Dora Demick

Chapter 55

Grandchild Grief

Anna lost her grandson the first week in September, 1975. It was Eddy, Stella's boy. He was 22 years old. His hobby of collecting animal traps led him to a convention in the Adirondack Mountains in the state of New York. Eddie had turned on the hibachi in his camper to cook his evening meal and then had turned down the windows about 4 inches on either side. He was looking over his purchases of the day. The fumes overtook him and he slowly went to sleep. It was a terrible tragedy. Stella was overwhelmed with grief. Eddy had been a good son. He reminded Stella of her brother Bill a great deal. Like Bill, Eddy had been a very special person too.

For two months she cried herself to sleep and could not have survived except for her husband Lyle. He comforted her and was always there for her when she needed him. It was during one of her sleepless nights that it suddenly dawned on Stella. She thought of her childhood. The days she would lie on the ground, her small body pressed close to the earth and sob her little heart out. Therein lay the answer as to why she cried so much. The grief she was to endure preyed upon her even as a child and the sorrow she would have in her heart for the loss of her beloved son.

One day Stella told Lyle that she wished to get back to the church. She had this strong need to be able to pray to God and ask his forgiveness. Lyle was very encouraging and so Stella called Anna and asked her about it. Anna was very pleased and said she would speak to her parish priest about it. A few days later, Stella called Anna again and

Anna told her that the parish priest had advised her that "Stella had made her bed and now must lie in it". Anna was upset that she could not be of more help.

Stella tried a few other churches in Toronto. The priests she spoke to had virtually the same thing to say as Anna's priest. It was not very encouraging. Lyle, seeing Stella's frustration, finally asked Stella what would happen if he should convert to Catholicism. Stella was in awe. He would do this for her! Lyle picked out a church from the telephone directory and called the priest. His name was Father O'Mara. Lyle spoke with the priest and Father O'Mara was appraised of the circumstances surrounding the death of Stella's son. The priest told Lyle to call him back in a few days and arrangements would be made for an interview.

A few days later, Lyle once more called the priest and again, was advised that he should contact the priest in a week's time. Lyle felt that he was being put off deliberately. But a week later he called Father O'Mara again. This time the priest arranged for an appointment to meet with Lyle and Stella for an interview. He explained to Lyle that one did not rush into this sort of thing too quickly and he wanted to give Lyle a chance to think about it seriously for a couple of weeks.

When they arrived for their interview, both were pleasantly surprised. Father O'Mara was a down to earth person and spoke very casually with them. They were to come down twice a week for six weeks to take instructions. By this time winter had set in and it was cold but they continued their lessons. Lyle had many questions to ask of the priest and Father O'Mara was pleased with Lyle.

One day he advised Stella and Lyle that it was time to make arrangements for Lyle's conversion. He had to be conditionally baptized first because Lyle had no proof of baptism. He would need a Godmother and a Godfather. Anna was staying at Johnny's place for Christmas when Stella finally got in touch with her. Stella brought Anna up to date on what had transpired and Anna at once insisted that she and Johnny be the Godparents to Lyle.

Arrangements had been made for one Saturday afternoon. Lyle and Stella had been to confession and everything was in readiness. When Lyle and Stella woke up that Saturday morning, they were shocked to see the blizzard outside. Stella telephoned Johnny and wondered about a cancellation. It was a sixty mile trip to Toronto and in the storm it was hard to say if any of the roads would even be open. Johnny advised Stella that Anna insisted on coming even in the storm.

There were cars stuck at the side of the road all the way into Hamilton. Anna pulled out her rosary and continued to pray out loud. She insisted that the devil himself was out to stop the conversion of Lyle but that they had God on their side and they would make it into Toronto for the four o'clock appointment. Stella and Lyle were very concerned about their arrival and imagined them being stuck at the side of some road in the blowing snow. They listened to the weather forecasts and heard the roads were so bad with snowdrifts that the snowploughs had difficulty getting through.

Anna continued to pray out loud and Johnny was amazed. It truly was a miracle. They managed to get through and arrived safely at Stella's place. No one had any time for refreshments and they proceeded to the church for the four o'clock appointment. When they arrived and told Father O'Mara where Anna and Johnny came from that day, he couldn't believe it. He told Stella to make some tea for her mother and Johnny in the church kitchen before they commenced with the baptism. It was a very special kind of ceremony. Lyle was baptized and took his oaths. He was now a Catholic and Stella was reunited with the church again. After the ceremony Anna and Johnny stayed the night at Stella's. The next day the roads were cleared and they proceeded on their trip back to Johnny's place in Port Dover.

Father O'Mara advised Stella not to tell anyone of her conversion back to the church, as people were cruel and sometimes would not understand. Anna was very pleased and called Lyle "her son". A couple of months later, Father O'Mara was transferred to another church and then the announcement appeared in the Toronto newspaper. Father O'Mara had been appointed the new Bishop of Thunder Bay.

Edward Duschl 1953-1975

Chapter 56

Big Toe Tale

One day after Lyle had retired, he and Stella decided to sell their home in Toronto and purchase a retirement home in cottage country. Their house sold very quickly and they purchased a home on a river in Huntsville. It was a big house and they enjoyed the privacy they had in the small town. The year was 1978. Anna was now 90.

Stella's son Gary called them at four o'clock in the morning and he was very serious. It was a terrible time for Stella. Gary announced that his brother Jim was deathly ill. Stella had just lost a son three years ago and her heart was breaking for her son Jim. His father had called the ambulance for Jim because he had become very weak. When the ambulance arrived, they took his temperature and established that it was 105 degrees. They immediately packed him with ice before they would move him and then took him to the hospital in Burlington. They had taken all sorts of tests to try to determine what was wrong with Jim. They were stumped. The high temperature was having its effect on Jim's memory. He was having memory lapses.

Stella and Lyle arrived at the hospital. Anna arrived at the same time and they were all shocked. Jim had lost so much weight and he looked so thin and fragile. Stella began to cry and she asked Jim where he was hurting. Jim said he had terrible chest pains. Anna was very concerned for her grandson. She sat at the foot of Jim's bed. The nurse took Stella aside and asked her questions about her son. Had he ever been this sick before? Did he usually have memory lapses? Stella answered no to both questions. The nurse advised that the hospital staff was very concerned because they did not know what had caused his illness.

Stella returned to Jim's bed. Anna lifted up the sheet and caressed Jim's foot slowly. He winced when she touched his big toe. Stella asked Jim if his foot was hurting him. He said that his big toe was very tender. Stella gasped and immediately thought of blood poisoning. She asked her son what had happened to his toe. Jim explained that a couple of weeks previously, he and some friends had gone fishing on Georgian Bay in Parry Sound. They, at one point had decided to go swimming and Jim had stubbed his big toe on a rock and it began to bleed. He had ignored it and it slowly became infected. He had treated it and the swelling had slowly gone away. He had completely forgotten about it and did not associate it with his illness at all. Stella immediately called the nurse she had been talking to and discussed the situation with her.

After Stella and her mother had left the hospital, the doctors rallied around and performed some further tests on Jim. This was Sunday afternoon. The family received a telephone call from the hospital. Jim was moved to the Hamilton General Hospital and his operation was scheduled for Monday morning at ten o'clock by a heart specialist.

Stella called her mother and explained to Anna the situation. Anna had discovered the problem by touching Jim's toe. Apparently after Jim had stubbed his toe and cut it, an alien virus had entered his blood stream. It was a virus which attacked the weakest part of the heart system. The family had not known, but Jim had a problem with his heart valve and this is what was being eaten up by the virus. Jim's heart valve was in such bad shape that it was like that of an 80 year old man.

The family had gathered at the hospital. He was transferred to the Hamilton General and the operation had begun immediately at ten o'clock that morning. Stella stayed with her son in the preparation room until surgery. She talked to Jim and he was barely conscious. He was in such terrible pain, only his eyes moved.

For almost three hours the family waited for the results of the surgery. Finally it was over. The doctor appeared at the doorway and advised that the operation had been a complete success. Jim had received a pigskin valve to replace his own and he was now in the intensive care unit. The family could see him just as soon as he was properly connected to the various apparatus.

When Stella entered the intensive care unit, her heart was broken again. Jim looked so pathetic as he lay there. All these tubes and wires were connected to his nose, mouth and chest. He was still out of it and Stella cried as she looked at her son. There was still a danger to his survival and she prayed to God that he would be strong enough to make it. Slowly a week went by and Jim was improving. The doctor advised that the worse was over and that Jim was now on the road to recovery. Jim was twenty four years old and his operation was only months after his first son Brandon was born.

It had been a terrible time for all the family. Anna was advised of the improvement of her grandson and she was thankful to God for his blessings. Somehow, she had been responsible for finding the solution to her grandson's illness and Stella was very grateful to her mother. Anna was now 90 years old.

Jim Duschl and Son Brandon

Chapter 57

Hotel For Sale

Anna decided that she wanted to go to Flin Flon to see Andrew. She had met this lady at the church. She was a much younger woman than Anna. They became very good friends and Anna liked her very much. One day Anna suggested to the woman that she should accompany her on a trip to Flin Flon. Since Anna was paying for it, the woman agreed and they took off for the mining town. Andrew had been divorced by now and a settlement had been reached between his ex wife and himself. She had taken their daughter and her son with her and he missed his little girl. Andrew put Anna and her friend up in his hotel in a room upstairs next to his own room. They stayed there in the hotel for over a week. Anna was satisfied that Andrew was doing well and she left Flin Flon with a clear conscience.

Anna had tried to talk Andrew into selling his hotel and moving to Hamilton with her. Andrew said that he would seriously consider it and let her know. Anna had planted the seed and she hoped and prayed that he would do her bidding. He was the only one left that she worried about because he was so far away from the rest of the family. She needed him to be close to her and she told him so.

Johnny would bring Anna to his place quite often. She needed a change and it was good for her to get away from the crowded apartment. Johnny and Teddy now had a daughter and Anna enjoyed her and thought that she was a beautiful child

The family worried about Anna though. She was over ninety years of age and she was getting to be forgetful sometimes. She would turn on the gas to heat the water for tea and then she would forget to turn it off. The girls contacted Anna on a daily basis to check up on her. Anne would come and visit as often as she could. They had built their new home in Grimsby. It was a large place and she and Tom were very happy together.

One day a few months later, Stella received a sobering telephone call from her daughter Adele. Jessie's husband Steve had passed away. He had a goitre and the doctors had it removed. Within a week he returned home from the hospital but he was not well. He was still working at the hotel and did not complain about anything. One day he just fell over on the floor and Jessie called Johnny who came over as soon as he could. He found Steve on the floor white as a sheet and called the ambulance. Steve was pronounced dead on arrival at the hospital. Apparently the goitre had been malignant and he had cancer of the throat, which the doctors had not detected. He had been in terrible agony towards the end. He died on August 29, 1980.

Jessie was devastated. Anna worried about her daughter. She had not been well herself. Jessie really took Steve's death hard. She was heart broken over her loss and was hospitalized. Eventually, Jessie was released from the hospital, sold her house and her daughter found her an apartment in a nicer area of Hamilton. Jessie furnished the place with her own furniture and appeared to be on the road to recovery.

Fred's wife was not feeling very well. She was having heart problems. She had a lung and heart operation a few years back and was very fragile. Fred worried about his wife and catered to her every need. His business was doing fine but he decided to sell it. This left him more time to spend with his wife. He purchased a Winnebago and they did quite a bit of travelling together.

One day, Fred brought Mary and his son Fred with them to Stella's place. They spent three days there and enjoyed the river and the meals Stella prepared for them. Their son brought his guitar with him and they played and sang songs. Everyone had a good time.

Andrew wrote and advised Anna that he had sold his hotel and would be coming back to Hamilton to live with Anna. Could she accommodate him? Anna arranged for a cot to be installed in the small kitchen and was prepared for his arrival. Andrew had received a good price for the hotel and was also getting a good price for his house. Anna was 92 years old and was still very spry and active. She looked forward to Andrew's arrival. Fred insisted that she stay at his place until such time as Andrew would arrive from Flin Flon. Anna agreed and they awaited Andrew's homecoming.

Stella Kuzyk Noble and Her Mother Anna

Chapter 58

More Heartbreak

Andrew finally arrived at Fred's place. Anna was very happy to see him and made plans on them moving back to her own apartment in Hamilton. Andrew had gained a lot of weight and was drinking pretty heavy. He was into the hard stuff. Canadian Club was his favourite. Fred would go out and purchase a couple of bottles, they would mix it with hot honey and kill the entire bottle in one day. They would sit and talk all day long and made plans to have Anna taken to a nursing home.

One day they took Anna to visit with his wife's mother who was in a nursing home. Anna became very agitated and told them she would never go to a nursing home as long as she lived. She had this thing about nursing homes and she wanted no part of it. She had all these children and now they were planning to place her in a home!

Fred and Andrew decided to call Stella and tell her to come and visit her mother. Fred called and said that her mother was not feeling very well and wanted to see her. The following Tuesday, Stella and her husband Lyle arrived in Burlington at Fred's place. She was surprised and happy to see Andrew. Stella went upstairs to visit with Anna. She was just fine and complained to Stella about her sons and their drinking. Stella was surprised about the whole matter.

Fred and Andrew wanted Stella to ask her mother if she would go to a nursing home where Fred's mother-in-law stayed. Not knowing anything about the way Anna felt about nursing homes, Stella said sure she would ask her mother. If it was as nice as they said it was, why would Anna object? Up the stairs went Stella. She started to explain to Anna that it might be the best thing for her if she would enter a nursing home. The doctors and nurses would always be there in case she needed them. She would have her food prepared for her and most of all, her children would visit with her on a daily basis. She would never be lonely. Anna flew into a rage. She was 93 years old but she was still very aware of what was going on. She immediately asked Stella if Fred and Andrew had put her up to it. Stella admitted that they did. No one brought the matter of nursing homes up again to Anna after that. Anna returned to her own apartment and Andrew moved in with her. At least she now had someone with her at all times. This relieved some of the pressure the other children were feeling about leaving Anna at home alone.

Andrew and Michael became very good friends. They started to go to the local hotel every night. Everyone at the hotel got to know the two brothers. They were drinking buddies. They spent a lot of time with Anna though and she was content to have them with her even if they were drinking. Michael would come to see his mother daily and Andrew would pour him a drink. They would laugh and talk to Anna and she provided them with food. The three of them were good for each other.

Mary's great granddaughter was getting married. Teresa had met a young man and they fell in love. It was to be a big wedding. The date had been set for July 14, 1984. The girls dressed Anna up in a fancy dress for the occasion. Anna was 96 years old. It was a lovely affair and everyone rallied around Anna. She got as much attention as the bride did. Michael escorted Anna to the head table to present the bride and groom with money in the plate. This time Anna did not sing to the happy couple. Everyone took pictures of Anna as well as the bride and groom. It was a day to remember.

The following spring, Fred's wife became very ill. They rushed her to the hospital. Her heart gave out on her and she died on May 1, 1985.

Fred was overwhelmed with grief. He had truly loved his wife and she produced him a son which was all they had ever wanted. Anna was 97 years old and would be burying a daughter-in-law. She attended at the funeral. It was a very sad occasion for the entire family.

Fred and Wife Mary Kuzyk

Chapter 59

Even More Heartbreak

Things were getting to be too much for Andrew. He would occasionally bring a girl home and Anna would object strenuously about it. She did not like Andrew bringing his girlfriends home to her place. Sometimes, if she liked the girl, she would not say anything. Andrew was over seventy years old but was still pretty active. Andrew decided that the rest of the family had to take their turns in looking after Anna.

He drew up a schedule of two week increments for each of the family. Anna could stay with Pauline for two weeks. Then she could stay with Anne a couple of weeks. Sonia could also take her turn and so could Stella. It worked out pretty well at first, but then Anna did not want to stay for two weeks at anybody's place. She wanted to come home sooner. Andrew was very frustrated. He had made plans and Anna would disrupt those plans.

Michael had not been over to visit Anna and Andrew for a couple of days and they both missed him. Anna told Andrew to go over to Michael's apartment and check up on him. It had been a very hot summer and the apartments got pretty unbearable at times. Andrew had tried to telephone Michael, but there was no answer. So Andrew went over to Michael's apartment. He knocked on the door and there was no answer either. Andrew had a key to Michael's apartment and he let himself in. Michael was lying on the bed on his back. He was very still and cold to the touch. Andrew was in a state of shock. He closed the door behind him and hurried back to Anna's place. He told Anna that he thought Michael was dead. Anna screamed and began to wail. She told Andrew to call the police.

The police investigated and it was determined later by the doctors that Michael had sugar diabetes and he had succumbed to a heart attack. They determined that he had died on September 26th, 1985. He was 72 years old. Anna had buried still another son. It was her eldest and she mourned deeply for him. He had always visited her and kept her company all those many years. They had become very attached to one another and looked after each other. Now he was gone.

After Anna had buried her son Michael, she became more mellow. She kept repeating over and over that it was soon her time to die. She wished for it to happen. She said that Peter had predicted that she would live to be over 100 years old so now she awaited that day and thought about the 2 years she still had to go before God would take her. She truly believed this.

Michael's granddaughter Michelle, had a son Michael born on April 7, 1986, just before Anna's 98th birthday. Anna had become a great great grandmother.

Anna went to stay at Anne's place for a while. Anne would prepare her special type of food. She would place it into containers and freeze them. This carton would hold many of these containers and all one had to do was thaw it out and Anna would have her special soup. Anne went to a great deal of trouble in preparing these soups for Anna. This carton with the containers followed Anna everywhere she went.

Soon it was Johnny's turn to keep Anna. Teddy would look after Anna like a daughter would and this pleased Anna very much. She truly loved her daughter-in-law. Johnny too was very good to his mother and catered to her every whim.

At last Andrew was getting a little bit of a rest. He would keep Anna in the apartment with him a week in between her visits. He did not mind this though and the family understood his need for a rest from

Anna. Anna stayed at Pauline's place for a couple of weeks. Then she spent some time with Sonia. She was sure getting the tour of the places.

Then it was Stella's turn to take Anna for a couple of weeks. Lyle and Stella had moved to Thornbury. He and Stella would drive to Hamilton and pick up Anna to stay with them a couple of weeks. These were long and tedious trips for Anna and she became very tired.

While at Stella's, Anna enjoyed her home made soups. Stella would put a chicken wing in the soup, together with some parsnip and noodles and Anna really enjoyed this. Stella would make it for her on a daily basis. She would also bathe Anna every morning and Anna enjoyed her sponge bath. Stella would rub her back with rubbing alcohol and relax her. Then she would have her soup for lunch and fall asleep in the afternoon.

Later when she awakened, Stella would bring her knitting in with her and sit and chat with Anna for a while. Anna would call all her children while she was at Stella's. She did not realize that it was long distance, but Stella did not mind and let her call whoever she wanted whenever she wanted.

One day early in the morning, she wanted to speak to Johnny. So Stella dialled the number and caught Johnny and Teddy just before they had to go to work. Stella apologized to Johnny and explained that Anna had insisted on it. He spoke briefly with Anna and she was satisfied for the rest of the day.

Suddenly one day, Anna decided that she wanted to go home to Andrew again. The two weeks were not yet up and Stella did not know what to do. She called Andrew and explained the situation to him. Anna was adamant and said she had to go home to her own apartment. So Andrew agreed to be home when they brought Anna back. It was a long and tiring trip for Anna. She was very upset and could not wait to get home. She kept asking how much further. At long last they arrived in Hamilton. Between Lyle and Stella, they managed to get Anna up the stairs and down the hall into her own apartment. Andrew was waiting for them. It was a relief for all of them, particularly Anna. She was old and tired and wanted to be where things were familiar to her. Andrew was again responsible for his mother and he accepted that responsibility.

Anna with Her First Great Great Grandchild

Chapter 60

Anna's Final Farewell

Anna was 99 years old when she finally agreed to go to a nursing home. Anne found the nursing home almost across the road from where she lived in Grimsby and assured Anna that she would come to visit her daily.

Anna had become weak and forgetful at times when she was making her tea and there was great concern that she might come to some harm when Andrew was not there. Andrew had been staying in the apartment with Anna but he was not always at home either. When she vacated the apartment to go to the nursing home, Andrew took over the lease and continued to live in the apartment. The children would come and visit her in the nursing home. She received her medication and everything appeared to run quite smoothly. Anne would visit Anna on a daily basis, sometimes twice a day depending on what her schedule was.

It happened during the winter months. Tom had retired from teaching and he and Anne made arrangements to go to Florida for the winter months. Anna began to miss her daughter and her visits. She became very moody and refused to take her medication. This created a great deal of problems for the staff at the nursing home. They decided to put her medication in her food. Anna knew something was up and refused to eat. She was causing the resident doctor to take desperate measures. They placed Anna in another room on the third floor with the Alzheimer patients. Anna was very unhappy about the move. One of the patients would come over to Anna's bed and start pinching her continually. Anna would scream for the nurses who would come running to see what the matter was. The doctor told Anna that she would have to be put on IV if she did not eat. She would not budge. They contacted the next of kin and then proceeded to attempt to feed her. Anne's daughter contacted her mother in Florida and Anne returned home as quickly as possible.

Anne was very concerned about her mother. She attended with the doctor and the staff and tried to reason with them about the medication. They had several meetings to see if a compromise could be reached to satisfy both the staff and Anna. Anne spoke to Anna and begged her to take her pills. Anna finally agreed to do as Anne asked and Anne reassured her that she would have her daughter come down to visit with Anna in her absence. Anna eventually became accustomed to Anne being away in Florida for the winter months and looked forward to spring and Anne's return. She missed her Anne very much.

The following May, the children decided to give Anna a 100th birthday party. They rented a club house in Hamilton. Everyone brought some food for the occasion. All the grandchildren and three great great grandchildren attended. Anna was brought to the party in a wheel chair as she was growing very weak. They filled up the club house and everyone ate. Anna sat at the head table with her children and each honoured her in their short speeches. She had a big birthday cake and blew out her candles. It was an occasion to be remembered.

Later everyone took pictures and Anna was featured in the newspaper as being 100 years old. She was getting very tired and they drove her back to the nursing home later. Anna was pleased about the party, but was glad to get back to the peace and quiet of the nursing home. The excitement was getting to be too much for her, and had made her very tired.

It was November 1989 when Stella and Lyle drove to the nursing home to see Anna. Stella was very surprised when she entered the room where Anna was staying. She was lying down on the bed, her head on the mattress and the pillow was covering her feet. She looked so small and cold. Stella tried to find something to cover her with but there were no blankets in the room. Anna awakened and asked who was there and Stella made herself known to her mother. Her eyes were bad and she could only see a slight blur. They chatted a few minutes and they hugged each other. Anna told Stella that she loved her and Stella needed to hear that. That night when Stella returned home, she started immediately on an afghan for her mother. She had a lot of blue wool so she double knitted the afghan to make it thick and warm. She was done with it in a couple of weeks.

Stella and Lyle set out once more to see Anna at the nursing home. It was snowing and blowing and driving conditions were not good. Stella wanted to see her mother nonetheless. When she arrived to the room, Anna was once more lying down and asleep. She did not awaken and Stella did not disturb her. Stella lovingly covered her mother with the afghan. She stayed for a while and watched Anna as she slept. When she did not wake up, Stella went to the desk and checked with the staff. They advised her that Anna was not feeling very well of late and slept a great deal.

It started to affect Anna just before Christmas. She was now 101 years old. Sonia took Anna to her place for Christmas and she was very weak at that point. She started to fade very rapidly after that. They rushed her to the hospital and notified Johnny in Port Dover. Anne and her husband returned from Florida. Things were not looking too good for Anna. Everyone rushed over to the hospital to see her. She was very frail looking and the nursing staff had placed her on IV. Every time she was connected, Anna would yank it out. The hospital staff gave up on it entirely. Anna knew it was getting close to her time

She kept saying something about her mother and that it was time for her to be placed in the hole. She was constantly attended by one or more of the children. The grandchildren also came to see her and to pay their respects. She was very weak and frail. The doctor was amazed to see her still alive. For some reason Anna seemed to want to hang on, yet the family knew that she was ready to die.

Anne called the parish priest and he came down to administer the last rights. Still Anna was in a turmoil. She kept calling out to "Mary" to leave her alone. She kept repeating it over and over. The other children brought Mary. They asked her to make her amends with her mother and she did several times. Still Anna kept repeating the same words for Mary to leave her alone and still she could not die.

Then Pauline remembered that there was a Mary from the church who had befriended Anna. They used to visit each other. She was a much younger woman and used to clean the church for the parish priest. She and Anna had a confrontation with each other some years back and the woman had called Anna a witch among other things. Anna had retaliated in like fashion and they had gone their separate ways. Pauline insisted that they go to fetch this Mary and bring her to the hospital so that Anna could make her peace with her. Anne knew where she lived and they drove over to see this Mary.

At first the woman refused to attend and said no way. Pauline and Anne begged her to come to see Anna. Pauline started to cry and pleaded with the woman. They said that Anna could not die in peace until she had been forgiven for some of the things that they said to each other years ago. The woman finally agreed and came to the hospital. She sat by the bed and made her peace with Anna. That night Anna passed away peacefully in her daughter's arms. It was as it should be that she died in Anne's arms. It was January 23, 1990 at approximately ten p.m. in the evening. Anna was in her one hundred and second year.

When Anna passed she was survived by 10 children, 31 grandchildren, 45 great grandchildren and 3 great great grandchildren. She had a full and extraordinary life, giving up so much of that life for her loved ones. All of her many descendants owe their very existence to Anna and her love, life and legacy have inspired these generations after her. Although she was small in stature, she had the strength of a giant. She will be eternally remembered by her descendants for her unselfish deeds as a beautiful, wonderful, remarkable and grand lady that she was.

Anna's 100th Birthday Party

CPSIA information can be obtained
at www.ICGtesting.com
Printed in the USA
LVHW070815240221
679597LV00040B/683

9 781632 215178